Travelling with Tech (iPhone/iPad Edition)

© 2023 iTandCoffee

Who is iTandCoffee?

iTandCoffee is an Australian-based small business established in 2012, offering technology support and education – for personal and small business technology. Our books are generally have corresponding classes and videos on the same topic.

The focus of iTandCoffee has always been on providing patient, friendly and supportive assistance – acknowledging that technology is a daunting and mystifying subject for so many people.

While iTandCoffee has always had a strong focus on Apple devices, we also provide assistance with, and training on, a wide range of other technology topics, including Android, Windows, Microsoft 365 and other cloud products, and much more – for home, and in business.

iTandCoffee operates in and around Camberwell, Victoria (in Australia), and also offers support and training remotely - both nationally and worldwide.

Visit www.itandcoffee.com.au to learn more about iTandCoffee.

Subscribe to the iTandCoffee newsletter at www.itandcoffee.com.au/newsletter.

Become an iTandCoffee member at www.itandcoffee.com.au/itandcoffee-club.

iTandCoffee Products and Services

For queries about iTandCoffee products and services – including our books, videos, newsletter, appointments, classes, membership and more - call **1300 885 420** (Australia only) or email **enquiry@itandcoffee.com.au**.

Travelling with Technology (iPhone/iPad Edition)

TABLE OF CONTENTS

Travelling with Technology (iPhone/iPad Edition)

TABLE OF CONTENTS

Travelling with Technology (iPhone/iPad Edition)

TABLE OF CONTENTS

Travelling with Technology (iPhone/iPad Edition)

TABLE OF CONTENTS

Travelling with Technology (iPhone/iPad Edition)

TABLE OF CONTENTS

Travelling with Technology (iPhone/iPad Edition)

TABLE OF CONTENTS

1. About this Book

This book has been developed based on research and planning that I have been doing for a trip that my husband and I will be taking later in 2023 – research and preparations that I figured would be worth sharing with others, as I know some of the topics relating to travelling with technology can be confusing and daunting.

The book looks at general travel considerations relating to technology that are independent of the type of mobile device that you take.

It also looks at specific apps, settings and features relating to the iPhone (and iPad) – specifically, those that apply under iOS 16. In places, it also refers to the Apple Watch.

The topics discussed in this book do assume at least a basic understanding of mobile phones and tablets - things like SIM cards providing access to the mobile phone and data network, and the difference between using Wi-Fi and mobile data for internet usage by a mobile device.

If you need further grounding on these concepts, refer to the iTandCoffee books **Getting Connected** (see www.itandcoffee.com.au/store/c180/technology-basics) and **Introduction to the iPad & iPhone – A Guided Tour** (see www.itandcoffee.com.au/store/c194/ios-intro-guided-tour-pb).

This **Travelling with Technology** book does not seek to provide any definitive advice on 'must-dos' and 'must-haves'. Instead, it provides suggestions, ideas, and alternatives to consider. It is certainly not intended to be an exhaustive study of this topic.

Most importantly, all readers must understand their own service provider's offering in relation to mobile services abroad – in terms of any costs, limitations and conditions associated with these services.

For readers who are from countries other than Australia, you will notice that the references to International Roaming in this book are about Australian Telco's.

Similar offerings are most like available for Telcos in your own country. Check their websites for details.

Anyone requiring one-on-one assistance or advice in relation to this topic (or any other technology topic) can contact iTandCoffee at **enquiry@itandcoffee.com.au**.

Or visit the iTandCoffee website at www.itandcoffee.com.au/appointment-request.html.

2. A Handy Checklist

Let's start with a summarised checklist of list of key things to consider before you travel.

Each of these items will then be explored in further detail throughout the book. The relevant chapter references are shown for each item in the list.

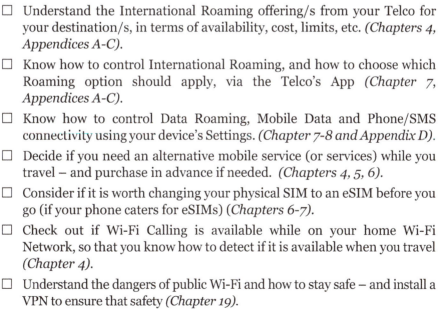

- [ ] Understand the International Roaming offering/s from your Telco for your destination/s, in terms of availability, cost, limits, etc. *(Chapters 4, Appendices A-C).*

- [ ] Know how to control International Roaming, and how to choose which Roaming option should apply, via the Telco's App *(Chapter 7, Appendices A-C).*

- [ ] Know how to control Data Roaming, Mobile Data and Phone/SMS connectivity using your device's Settings. *(Chapter 7-8 and Appendix D).*

- [ ] Decide if you need an alternative mobile service (or services) while you travel – and purchase in advance if needed. *(Chapters 4, 5, 6).*

- [ ] Consider if it is worth changing your physical SIM to an eSIM before you go (if your phone caters for eSIMs) *(Chapters 6-7).*

- [ ] Check out if Wi-Fi Calling is available while on your home Wi-Fi Network, so that you know how to detect if it is available when you travel *(Chapter 4).*

- [ ] Understand the dangers of public Wi-Fi and how to stay safe – and install a VPN to ensure that safety *(Chapter 19).*

2. A Handy Checklist

☐ Prepare your devices by turning off mobile options that could unintentionally use data (unless you are not concerned about data usage) *(Chapter 8)*

☐ Make sure your device has enough storage for all your travel data, apps, photos – delete/offload unwanted apps & data *(Chapter 9)*

☐ Is the device's battery OK? Does it need replacing? Do you need to take a portable charger? *(Chapter 9)*

☐ Have all available software updates been applied? *(Chapter 9)*

☐ Pre-download necessary apps, translations, maps, city guides *(Chapter 16, 17, 20)*

☐ Get the apps associated with all your flights, accommodation, bookings, tickets, etc. *(Chapters 13, 14, 15, 17, 20, 21)*

☐ Get your itinerary into digital format – all stored so that internet is not required *(Chapter 15)*

☐ In advance, test out the messaging and internet calling apps you will be using with the key people with whom you will need to have contact while travelling *(Chapter 10-12)*

☐ Pack those travel accessories, adaptors, charges, cables – including a SIM pin (extractor) if needed *(Chapter 18)*

☐ Money – will you use a travel debit card? Get the app/s, know how to load currency, consider pre-loading when exchange rate is good. Get a currency conversion app. Set up exchange rate alerts. Notify your bank of your travel plans *(Chapter 21)*

☐ Think about your travel photos – will you be using iCloud? Do you have enough storage on your device and in iCloud? *(Chapter 22)*

☐ Check that your Camera app will store the location of the photos that you take *(Chapter 22)*

☐ Pre-load entertainment (movies, TV series, podcasts, books, audo books) *(Chapter 23)*

☐ Make sure **Find My** is enabled – and know how to find/lock/erase a lost device *(Chapter 19)*

☐ Make sure you know your Apple ID and password - in case you need to access Find My from someone else's device. *(Chapter 19)*

☐ Get those passwords into a form that is paperless! And make sure your iPad/iPhone has a good Passcode. *(Chapter 15 & 19)*

☐ Add Medical ID information to your iPhone, including emergency contacts *(Chapter 9)*

3. Keeping Connected when Travelling

First, what are your phone & text needs?

When considering your mobile phone and text requirements while travelling, there are some key questions to consider:

- Do people from home need to call you? How often?
- If yes, does it matter if they must phone you on an international number?
- Or do you need an Australian number to avoid high cost to those who call you from back home? Does this number need to be your usual mobile number?
- Will you need to call home? How often?
- Do you need a phone for local calls at your destination - to contact travel companions or to arrange tours, accommodation, etc.
- Do you need to send SMS's? How often?
- Are you travelling with someone else who will have phone/text access?
- And could you just survive with internet messaging and calling?

You may not need a phone service at all!

For many trips, no Phone / SMS capability is needed – or at least is rarely needed.

You can consider managing the whole trip using messaging and internet calling apps (e.g. Messages, Facetime, WhatsApp, Facebook Messenger) and (maybe) Wi-Fi Calling (something we'll cover soon).

All these methods of communication need is an internet connection – and this can be using free Wi-Fi at hotels and other accommodation, Airports, Cafes, and even sometimes while in transit on trains, in buses and other places.

3. Keeping Connected when Travelling

But best to never say never!

It is important to consider the scenario where you *do* need to make a phone call – perhaps a lengthy call – to back home.

What if your credit card gets blocked and you need to call your bank! Or there is the need to call someone in the country in which you are (or will be) travelling.

In the case of the bank, you could be left on hold for lengthy periods - so you need a phone service that won't cost a fortune for the amount of time you need to be on that call.

And is there a chance you might need to receive a text code to your usual number, to authorise a new payee or to sign-in to one of your online accounts? You will need your home SIM to be in your mobile device to receive such a text.

For your home mobile plan, what options do you have?

If you take your mobile phone with your home SIM, you can use something called **International Roaming**, which we'll talk about in more detail shortly.

Basically, it involves using your phone's usual SIM card when you travel for phone calls, SMSs, and mobile data – *at an extra cost*.

International Roaming may well be enabled by default for your mobile service, but you may need to check in advance (with your Telco) to make sure it is available and learn how to enable and (if needed) disable it.

Telco websites provide such information – or you can call or visit your Telco to discuss what is available to you.

The app associated with your mobile service will also usually show what International Roaming service is available. We discuss three Australian Telco apps in the Appendices.

3. Keeping Connected when Travelling

These days, International Roaming using your home mobile service usually takes the form of

- **Day packs/passes/add-ons** – a fixed daily or weekly charge covering calls and texts and a limited amount of mobile data; or perhaps a charge that covers a nominated period and provides an allowance of call minutes and mobile data for that period.
- **Pay As You Go (PAYG)**, where you pay by the minute for phone calls (both in <u>and</u> out), pay for each outgoing SMS, and pay for every MB of mobile data you use. This PAYG option can end up costing a fortune, especially if you use any mobile data or need to make long phone calls.

So you will need to understand what is available for the mobile plan you have with your Telco and for the location/s you will visit: what are the costs, conditions, restrictions, etc. and how you can control which option you will use (if more than one is available). We will discuss some available options for each of the three major Australian Telcos shortly.

Other Alternatives to using your home SIM/plan

If you discover that the charges associated with International Roaming using your home SIM will be too expensive or inadequate - or there are no packs/passes/add-ons available for your plan or destination - there may be other cheaper options available.

You may be able to pre-purchase an alternative SIM for your destination/s before you go.

This could be a Pre-Paid SIM with a 'roaming pack' from an Australian Telco.

Or you can get a special 'Travel SIM' that you purchase online, as either a physical SIM card or as something called an eSIM[1] (if your phone supports eSIMs).

---

[1] eSIM stands for embedded SIM and is a SIM card that is built in to your device – instead of a separate physical SIM that you insert. Devices with eSIM capability will allow multiple eSIMs to be added, although only two SIMs/mobile numbers can be active at any given time. iPhones since the iPhone XE and XS have included the eSIM capability, which is managed from Settings -> Mobile.

3. Keeping Connected when Travelling

Another option – which is often the cheapest, as long as you are staying long enough in each country – is to purchase a local SIM or eSIM at your destination. You may also be able to purchase a multi-country SIM at that destination (depending on where you are travelling).

Choosing the best solution for your own travels will depend on where you are going and what SIMs are available for these places, how long you are staying in each place, how contactable you need to be, how you feel about buying at your location, how comfortable you are with managing settings relating to phone and data usage, and a few other parameters.

We will look at these alternatives in more detail shortly, discuss some options, and look at why you might choose one over the other.

And what are your Internet needs?

In addition to your phone needs, you will need to consider your use of internet while you travel – for checking emails, looking up tours, messaging using apps, using mobile banking, entertainment, and so much more.

Will you only need/plan to use internet at your accommodation and/or use public Wi-Fi available at cafés, airports, and other places?

Or will you need mobile internet when you are away from Wi-Fi - for example, for navigation, translations, messaging and more when you going from place to place?

If you need mobile data on the go (away from Wi-Fi)

Why might you need internet away from Wi-Fi? If you want to

- use your phone for **navigation**, mobile internet is needed to refresh the maps as you move (unless those maps have been downloaded in advance).
- use **SIRI** – perhaps for translation or information about your location – you will need mobile internet.
- **translate** signs or converse in another language, you will need internet for these translations (unless you have downloaded translation files in advance).

3. Keeping Connected when Travelling

- **message** travel companions (or family/friends back home) while on the move – using internet messaging apps/features like iMessage, Whatsapp, Messenger, Telegram, Viber, etc – you will need mobile internet.
- **look up information** about the sights around you – and get directions to your next sight – you will need mobile internet.

If you think you might need internet on the go (when you are away from Wi-Fi), you will need a SIM card that has a **mobile data allowance** and that can access the mobile network available locally as you travel.

You will need to consider how often might you need the mobile internet, and how much data you might need (which will depend on the sorts of things you need to do).

All of these considerations will help determine which of the following options (one or more) might be best for accessing mobile internet as you travel:

- Use your usual SIM with International Roaming and *Data Roaming* (which we'll talk about in more detail soon).
- Pre-purchase a SIM or eSIM for your destination/s (a data-only SIM or with phone and text as well).
- Buy a local SIM or eSIM at your destination, one that has a data allowance.

Online Safety considerations

An important consideration when thinking about how you will access the internet during your travels is **staying safe online**.

Public Wi-Fi networks are notoriously unsafe. Even your hotel's Wi-Fi may not be completely safe.

Using your phone's SIM card to access the internet will always be safer than any public Wi-Fi network – so this may drive your decision around the best option for internet access during your trip.

We cover the topic of online safety on public Wi-F networks in more detail in a chapter 19.

4. Let's Talk International Roaming

We mentioned International Roaming in general in earlier pages, so let's now explore this in some more detail.

In particular, we will look at International Roaming using the three main Telcos in Australia – Telstra, Optus and Vodafone.

If you are a reader from a different country (or are using a SIM from a different Australian Telco), check with your own Telco to see what International Roaming products are available to you. They may well offer something similar to what is described here.

In fact, here is a handy article that provides a good overview of the Australian offerings at the time of writing this book: www.whistleout.com.au/MobilePhones/Guides/phone-plans-with-international-roaming.

What is International Roaming?

International roaming is a service that allows you to use your mobile phone when you travel outside of your home country, using the SIM card and mobile service that you normally use at home.

When you are in another country and your usual mobile network isn't available (i.e. there are no mobile towers belonging to your home country's service provider), International Roaming allows your mobile device to connect to mobile towers that belong to a partner network, one that has an agreement with your home service provider.

Extra costs are incurred for such connections, in addition to any monthly plan payment.

Controlling International Roaming

If you plan to take your home mobile service with you when you travel abroad (i.e. you plan to use your home SIM card), make sure you understand the International Roaming offering from your Telco – and how to enable or disable it.

For the major Australian Telcos, the International Roaming settings for the service can be managed from the Telco website, by signing into the account that you have set up with that Telco. But there is an easier way to manage the International Roaming settings associated with your mobile service/s – and that is from the Telco's App.

4. Let's Talk International Roaming

Get your Telco's App to Manage International Roaming

Make sure you install your Telco's app on your mobile device/s in advance of your trip, and make sure you have learned how to use it before you go.

We briefly discuss the apps for 3 major Australian Telcos in the Appendices – the **My Telstra**, **My Optus,** and **My Vodafone** apps.

Ensure that you know where to check and manage the International Roaming settings for your mobile service from within the applicable App.

The International Roaming features that are available for your mobile service will depend on the plan associated with that service – so also make sure you understand what your plan offers.

If your plan does not offer a suitable roaming service, you may need to consider making necessary changes to your plan, or consider using an alternative SIM or SIMs for your travels.

Also be alert to the fact that the International Roaming services, costs, and availability will depend on your travel destination – with some destinations not covered by the 'daily pass' type of roaming that we describe below, and/or perhaps incurring higher roaming costs.

Daily Pass / Pack / Add-on

Here's a summary of the Daily Pass/Pack/Add-on offering for each of the three main Australian Telco's. Refer to the Appendices for more information about each of these.

Telstra and Vodafone, a Day Pass/Pack is offered for a daily fee, for a range of destinations and plan at

- $10 per day for Telstra (OR only $5 if travelling in NZ) and
- $5 per day for Vodafone

4. Let's Talk International Roaming

where the daily charge is only incurred if any of these 3 events occur during a 24-hour period:

- you make or receive a phone call.
- you <u>send</u> an SMS.
- you access mobile data or send/receive an MMS.

Once the charge is triggered, this then provides you with unlimited calls and texts for that day. Receiving an SMS does not trigger the daily fee.

Important: Just be aware that for Telstra, the 'day' is a 24-hour period from 0:00-24:00 AEST, so you could easily incur 2 daily charges on the one day of use overseas. Vodafone customers should check if the same applies to its daily roaming product.

For Optus, you can specifically choose to enable a daily ($5) or 7-day ($35) 'pass' as and when it is needed. The 24 hours of the 'day' (or '7-days') starts as soon as the pass is purchased.

Once the Optus pass is enabled, you have unlimited calls and texts for those 24 hours (or 7 days). (Note. That you don't need to be on Wi-Fi to enable the pass.)

Each of the Telco's also provide mobile data as part of the day pass/pack/add-on.

For Telstra, you will have only 1GB of data for use in the 24 hours (0:00-24:00 AEST).

Optus offers a more generous 5GB for a single day pass, and 35GB for a 7-day pass.

Vodafone allows you to use your usual monthly data allowance as covered by your plan – which could be tens of GBs.

For all Telco's, additional charges apply if you exceed the data allowance.

Again, it must be emphasized that the cost, availability, and inclusions will depend on your plan and the destinations for your travel.

There may be a limit on the number of days of the year that you can use roaming day passes. Always check your Telco's website for further details.

And just a note for anyone who has a Belong SIM card in their phone: Belong has just announced its new International Roaming pack. For $30, it provides 3GB of data, unlimited texts and 150 minutes of calls, all valid for 15 days.

4. Let's Talk International Roaming

An important exclusion is that day passes/packs/add-ons will **not** be available on cruise ships – even when you are close to shore.

PAYG (see below) will apply for any mobile phone and data usage on the cruise, so beware!

Pay As You Go (PAYG)

As indicated by the name, this type of International Roaming means you will pay for

- every minute of an incoming or outgoing phone call (e.g. $1-$3 per minute)
- every text you send (e.g. 50¢ - 75¢ per text)
- every MB of mobile data you use ($1-$3 per MB).

Pay As You Go (PAYG) is certainly an excellent option to consider using if you just want to send a quick SMS on a given day – or perhaps make a really quick call.

However, if you ever do use the Pay As You Go type of International Roaming, make sure that you are **absolutely certain** that your Data Roaming is disabled in your device's Settings (covered in more detail in Chapter 7.).

Otherwise, you could incur hundreds - or even thousands - of dollars in mobile data charges.

What if you have a Pre-Paid service?

Different options and charges will apply if the mobile service you use is pre-paid. Check with your Telco about available International Roaming options (if any) for your pre-paid SIM.

For example, Telstra offers Pre-Paid Roaming Packs that include a certain number of minutes of calls, a certain number of SMSs and a data allowance. Such packs are valid for between 3 and 14 days. But not all destinations are covered.

Optus has similar options for single and 7-day periods, as well as offering 'Travel Credit' and a 'Data Only' option that is valid for 14 days.

Vodafone offers some Prepaid Roaming Add-on options covering periods from 1 to 7 days.

4. Let's Talk International Roaming

Again, check if your travel destination/s is/are covered.

See the Appendices A-C for more information about these options.

International Roaming vs Data Roaming

As already described, **International Roaming** refers to the provision of mobile phone, text, and data services by a partner network when you are not currently connected to your usual home Telco – and the type of International Roaming service you use from your Telco is managed from the Telco's app.

It is very important to understand that there is also a **Data Roaming** setting managed from your mobile phone's Settings.

This Data Roaming setting allows you to control whether your device uses the International Roaming offered by your Telco for mobile internet.

You can choose to just use the phone/text aspect of International Roaming, and not use the International Roaming for mobile data – since it is usually the use of mobile data roaming that causes unexpected (and often large) expense.

We will look further at the settings/controls for controlling phone, SMS and mobile data connectivity in chapter 7.

Note that similar considerations apply for any tablet that has an active SIM card for mobile data.

Using the eSIM in your Watch for Roaming

If you have an Apple Watch with an eSIM – one that you can use in Australia to access phone, text, and mobile data even when you do not have your iPhone with you – you may wonder if that eSIM will still work when travelling outside Australia.

International Roaming may not be available for your Apple Watch's eSIM.

4. Let's Talk International Roaming

This depends on your Telco, but for the Australian major Telco's, it doesn't appear to be an option at the time of writing this book.

As you travel, you can still use your Watch for taking calls, reading texts, tracking your steps, and all sorts of other things. You will just need to have your iPhone in Bluetooth range or be on Wi-Fi.

The Watch won't be able to be used independently of your iPhone for connectivity tasks, so keep your iPhone with you.

Wi-Fi Calling - A cost-free option for calls and texts to/from home

There is a relatively new feature of modern mobile phones that is important to understand, particularly in relation to travel.

It is something called **Wi-Fi Calling**, and only became available in the past few years.

Not all mobile phones and SIM cards offer or support it, and not all Wi-Fi networks or countries allow it.

But if it *is* available, it is worth considering its use when you travel – as it will let you call and text a number **in your home country** (or receive a call from home) without incurring any International Roaming costs. This includes being able to check your voicemail without incurring costs.

Wi-Fi Calling allows standard calls and texts using your home mobile service (SIM) to occur over Wi-Fi instead of using the mobile phone network. This is also known as VOIP (voice over internet protocol). Of course, you must be connected to Wi-Fi for this to work.

The **Wi-Fi Calling** setting is found in **Settings -> Mobile** on the iPhone (or in the Mobile settings for an individual SIM, if your phone has multiple SIMs).

Turn it on if you want to take advantage of this feature.

4. Let's Talk International Roaming

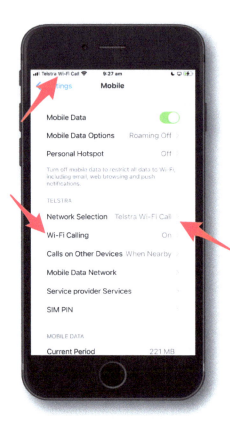

In the example on the left, the status bar at the top of the iPhone screen shows that Wi-Fi Calling is currently active - so the phone will use the connected Wi-Fi for calls and text messages **to and from Australian numbers,** instead of using the mobile network.

On an iPhone that doesn't have a Home Button, look in the Control Centre (swipe down from top right) to check if Wi-Fi Calling it is active (see image below).

Or go to **Settings -> Mobile** to see if it is turned on. The **Network Selection** field (see image on left) shows if it is currently active.

If, during your trip, your home SIM is currently active (which means Aeroplane/Flight mode must be off), you are connected to a Wi-Fi network, and you find that Wi-Fi Calling shows as being available, you will be able to call and text with **those back in your home country** without triggering any daily or PAYG International Roaming charge.

I will emphasise again that **only calls to/from your home country are free using Wi-Fi Calling via your home SIM card**.

Calls/SMS's that use your home SIM and that are made to/from any country other than your home (even the country in which you are currently travelling) cannot use Wi-Fi Calling and will instead need to use the local mobile network – so will trigger International Roaming charges.

The trick can be working out if Wi-Fi Calling is active, because you can't always guarantee it will be.

4. Let's Talk International Roaming

As mentioned above, it doesn't work on certain Wi-Fi networks, in certain locations - and your phone may not currently have it active for some other reason.

To check if it is available right now, make sure you are connected to a Wi-Fi network that has internet access and that Aeroplane/Flight mode is turned off.

If you expect it to be available but find it isn't, try turning Aeroplane/Flight mode on and back off again. Then wait a minute (or two or three) to see if it becomes available.

Importantly, for Wi-Fi calling to be available, **a VPN cannot be active**. (We'll talk more about VPNs, and why you might normally use one, in chapter 19.)

Note that if someone calls you after you turn off Aeroplane/Flight mode but before you have worked out if Wi-Fi Calling is currently available, you may incur a daily or PAYG charge if you answer the call.

Important Note: Just to re-enforce the points already made, Wi-Fi Calling is **not** supported when you are using a VPN and it only offers free calls and texts to/from numbers in your home country.

How to make a call locally while travelling

If you do need to place a phone call or send a text to a local (or not so local) number while you are travelling, you should always make sure to include the international code in front of the number. This code starts with a +, then a 2-3 digit number. (See Page 57 for more on how to type a + when dialling.)

If you are not sure of the international code for your current location, here is a website that allows you to look this up: countrycode.org.

For example, to dial a number in Portugal when using my home SIM, I will need to include +351 in front of any local Portuguese number.

Note that you may be able to place 'calls' to local numbers in your travel destination without a phone service, using internet calling apps like Whatsapp and Viber – if the person/business you are calling supports this. We'll talk about these apps further in chapter 11.

5. Use an Alternative SIM (or SIMs)

If the International Roaming option/s offered by your usual Telco are too expensive or inadequate, or perhaps don't provide an acceptable solution for your travel destination, there may be other options available for phone, text, and mobile data during your travels.

Pre-Purchasing a Travel SIM

One option is to pre-purchase a 'travel SIM' that covers one or more destination.

There are several important considerations when purchasing such a SIM:

- Do you need it to provide a phone/text service, or do you just need mobile data?
- If you need phone, do you want to have a mobile number from your home country, so that people from home can call you without incurring international call charges?
- Does your phone support eSIMs?
- If yes, are you prepared to use the eSIM feature?
- Do you want the purchased SIM to cover multiple destinations or just a single country.
- For any option you consider, does it provide good coverage for your destination (since not all SIMs and services are made equal).

For many travellers, mobile data is really all that is needed from a travel SIM – allowing messaging and calling using apps/internet, instead of using a mobile phone service.

There are lots of websites offering Travel SIMs, with options for phone and text service and/or mobile data.

And if you are prepared to venture into the world of eSIMs, you can purchase inexpensive eSIMs online or via an easy-to-use App.

Let's look at some of the options.

5. Use an Alternative SIM (or SIMs)

Websites for pre-purchasing Travel SIMs

There are various websites for pre-purchasing Travel SIMs and this book will not seek to recommend any of them. Rather, this chapter is intended to offer some suggestions for you to explore yourself. I have included some screen shots taken during my look at options for a trip to Europe (as an example).

- www.onesimcard.com.au – provides a SIM (or eSIM) that can have both an international and Australian mobile number.

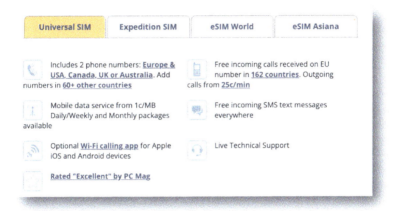

- www.simoptions.com – seems to give option of eSIM with phone/SMS service in, say, Europe – but delivery to Australia for physical SIMs looked expensive.

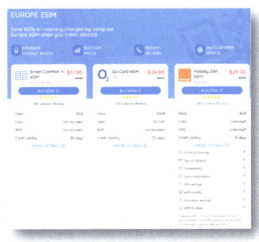

5. Use an Alternative SIM (or SIMs)

- simsdirect.com.au – both SIMs and data-only eSIMs

- simcorner.com

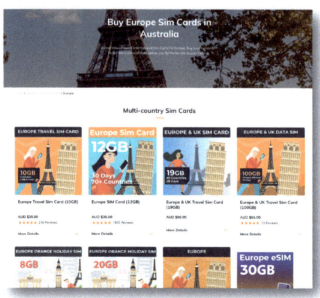

5. Use an Alternative SIM (or SIMs)

- prepaidsims.com.au

Which website should I use?

As already mentioned, this book does not seek to provide any recommendation on this. You will need to do your own research. Here's an online review that talks about Travel SIMs:

productreview.com.au/c/travel-sims

Just make sure you fully check and compare inclusions, costs, exclusions, and coverage for your travel destination before making your choice.

Another Option: Purchase SIM at destination

Purchasing a SIM at your destination will usually give the cheapest option for local calls and mobile data – and may provide larger data allowances than offered for International Roaming with your home provider and pre-purchased SIMs.

5. Use an Alternative SIM (or SIMs)

At some destinations (e.g. in Europe), you may be able to get a SIM that covers multiple countries.

For such a multi-country SIM, you will need to enable data roaming to use any mobile data for the SIM – as such a SIM will generally be associated with a particular country. Using it for mobile internet in the other eligible countries requires that data roaming is enabled. (More on controlling data roaming in chapter 7.)

Here is a checklist of things to consider in relation to purchasing a SIM at your destination.

❑ Research where/how you will buy the SIM - at the airport (often more expensive, less options), in the town, or electronically (for eSIMs).

❑ Calls to home are international calls – this may not be covered by the SIM plan, or could end up expensive (unless there is an allowance in the plan you purchase).

❑ Texts to home (international) may not be included.

❑ Be prepared to do some APN configuration in device's mobile settings when you install the SIM – and know where to do this. (This is covered in chapter 7.)

❑ Consider if this is really the best option if you are travelling to multiple countries, with short-ish stays in each. Will multiple SIMS be needed? Can you get a SIM at your destination that covers all the countries you will be visiting?

❑ There could be a potential language barrier when buying/setting up – so you many need a translation app (and downloaded language files to do translations without internet).

❑ You will most likely have to provide Passport details and may even have to provide a local address.

❑ Don't forget you may still need home your home SIM for receiving texts, checking voicemails, and making calls home.

5. Use an Alternative SIM (or SIMs)

My Preferred Option: Use an App to get a data eSIM

The option that I will be using when we next travel is to get a data-only eSIM that covers one or more of the countries in which I will travel.

I will still have my home SIM available for International Roaming, should I need it for phone calls and texts (which I will aim to only use very occasionally).

I have converted my usual home SIM to an eSIM, which means that I won't need to take it out and store it. I will just turn it off in my iPhone's settings when I don't want to use it. That SIM will have Data Roaming turned off, and this Data Roaming setting will only be enabled if I decide to use a 'day pass'.

My iPhone can host up to 8 eSIMs (with only 2 SIMS able to be active at any given time – i.e. the physical SIM and eSIM, or two eSIMs).

I will purchase and install the data-only eSIM for my first destination just before I leave, so that it is ready to use on my arrival at that destination.

I will use an App for this purchase, one that I have tested out and found works really well.

I will then use this data-only SIM during my trip to message and call friends and family, using a combination of iMessages, Facetime Whatsapp, and Facebook Messenger. I will also use it for navigation and translation.

If needed, I will purchase another one of these data-only eSIMs for other locations.

This will be far cheaper than paying over $300 for a month's International Roaming with Telstra.

Using an App to purchase an eSIM

If your mobile phone supports eSIMs, there is a handy app that makes it really easy to purchase a data-only eSIM for anywhere in the world.

It is called **Airalo** and it can be downloaded from the App Store.

5. Use an Alternative SIM (or SIMs)

It allows for the purchase of **Local eSIMs** for different countries, **Regional eSIMs,** and **Global eSIMs** (see options along the top of the screen in the image below, below the words **Hello, Lynette**).

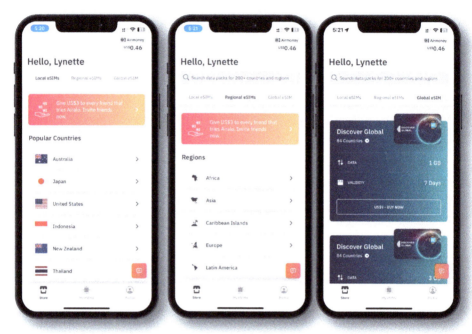

It is worth trying out this app first, before you go.

To do this, you can purchase a 7-day eSIM for here in Australia for only US$4.50. This SIM will use the Optus network.

After purchase, the app will install the eSIM for you – allowing you to see how the eSIM looks in your Mobile settings, and to see the settings for each SIM that you will need to manage while travelling.

We cover these settings in chapter 7 and then look at more detail about how to manage multiple SIMs in Appendix D.

6. Which Option/s Should I Choose?

With all of those options described above, let's take a bit more of a look at the option (or options) you might choose for phone and mobile internet when you travel, depending on your requirements.

I can afford the International Roaming pass/pack/add-on from my Telco

The easiest option for staying connected when you travel is to leave your home SIM card in your phone and take advantage of your Telco's roaming pass/pack/add-on, which usually takes the form of a daily fee that provides unlimited calls and texts and provides a specified data allowance.

If you can afford the cost of such a roaming service from your home Telco, this certainly avoids the hassle of purchasing and switching between SIM cards.

However, you may still need to know how to manage your usage of mobile data (and, perhaps, phone) to stay within whatever limits apply (see chapter 7).

I need my home number for calls and texts

If you must have access to your home mobile service for calls and texts while away, then you will have no choice but use International Roaming through your home Telco, utilising whatever roaming service they offer.

Consider that even using a daily roaming pack may end up being a very expensive option (depending on your Telco) if you are going on a longer trip.

6. Which Option/s Should I Choose?

For example, a 30-day trip roaming with Telstra would cost $300 (assuming the roaming is used every day and you choose their $10 daily roaming fee option). For Optus and Vodafone, the cost would be half that amount – so perhaps more affordable.

So, even if you need access to your home mobile service, you may want to still consider limiting how often you take advantage of any daily roaming - which means understanding how to control connectivity and only connecting to the mobile service at times that you know you need to use it.

If only PAYG is available for your plan/destination, you will need to be fully aware of the charges for calls and texts and how to prevent any data usage.

And if you need to make or receive a long call while on PAYG, you may be left with a big bill – so should really consider if you need an alternative to your home service as your backup plan.

International Roaming will be too expensive

Even if you decide that International Roaming through your home Telco is not your preferred option because of the cost, it is still a good idea to have access to this international roaming during your trip – even if you just use it very occasionally.

On most days, leave your phone in aeroplane/flight mode with Data Roaming & Mobile Data turned off - or even consider taking out (and safely storing) the physical SIM card (if applicable) to avoid any charges on that service. (And, of course, you'll need to make sure to take the little pin for popping out the SIM!)

Then, just use public and accommodation Wi-Fi instead of your mobile service.

If you have more than one SIM in the device, you must turn off each SIM to avoid any charges for each service – and only turn on the applicable SIM when you want to utilise its services. The **Data Roaming** and **Mobile Data** settings will need to be managed on a per SIM basis.

6. Which Option/s Should I Choose?

We'll cover all these connectivity settings in more detail from page 38 and in look at multiple SIMs in further detail in Appendix D.

Consider only using the 'daily pass' type of international roaming on days that you want to use it for several things, where you will get your money's worth. Otherwise, stay in Aeroplane/Flight Mode with data roaming and mobile data turned off.

Also consider that there may be the free option of **Wi-Fi Calling** when you are connected to Wi-Fi – which does not involve any roaming charges **if calls (or texts) are made to/from your home country** while this is active. We describe Wi-Fi Calling in more detail on page 23.

And if you do need to be contactable by phone while travelling but don't want to (or can't) use your home service, consider a pre-purchased travel SIM that covers your destination/s – a selection of which we cover earlier in chapter 5.

As described there, some such SIMs offer a local Australian phone number for the SIM (as well as an international mobile number) – so that those who call you will not have to dial an overseas number.

We have successfully used such SIMs on our own travels in the past because we had family members who needed to be able to call us as often as they liked without incurring additional costs.

I need a local phone number at my destination

If you need a local number at your travel destination, you will probably need to buy a SIM or eSIM at your destination. This is often the cheapest option for phone and data (unless you are going to lots of countries for short periods).

Note that you will only be able to use the option of an alternative SIM if your mobile phone is not locked to a particular home network. Those Australians travellers with iPhones will not have this issue, as recent iPhones are not locked in this way.

6. Which Option/s Should I Choose?

See page 29 for a checklist to consider in relation to purchasing at your destination.

As also covered from page 26, there may be the option of pre-purchasing a SIM for your specific destination/s before you travel.

But really consider what it is you need a local number for. Is it because you will need to make or receive lots of local calls?

Can you arrange things online? Is WhatsApp an option for locals to call you and you to call them?

And for the number of times you need a phone, might your home service's International Roaming and its daily charge be a cost-effective option?

I will definitely need mobile internet

As for phone/SMS access while travelling, the easiest option for mobile internet is often to just use your usual home SIM and the data roaming allowance offered by our Telco – if it provides sufficient data, and the cost is affordable.

If you don't want to use data roaming with your home SIM, or if the data offered for data roaming is insufficient, there is the option to get a separate SIM with a data allowance. If you don't need a phone service with this SIM number, this can be a data-only SIM.

If your phone supports it, consider the option of eSIM so that you don't have to remove your home SIM (but can instead just turn off the home SIM).

In fact, you might want to also consider converting your home SIM to an eSIM before you travel, so that the SIM tray is free for any physical travel SIM that you may want to purchase.

As described in chapter 5. , data-only eSIMs can be easily purchased online before you leave, as well as during your travels – via websites or an app.

6. Which Option/s Should I Choose?

And has been mentioned several times, if your home SIM is a physical SIM, make sure you take it with you as backup to any travel SIM you purchase and use, and don't forget the pin for popping out the SIM tray.

My trip will include lots of destinations

Consider an international SIM that covers the locations you are visiting. These can be purchased on arrival (depending on your destination), and some multi-country Travel/Tourist SIMs can be purchased in advance.

Or keep it simple by just using the International Roaming associated with your home SIM - if you can afford this, and it provides enough data allowance.

I will be cruising

It is important to note that the international roaming day passes/packs/add-ons that most Australian Telcos offer **do not cover cruising**, even if you are close to shore.

PAYG or special cruising packs may apply and can be very expensive.

Check with your Telco if you are not sure. Closely explore the option - and cost - of Wi-Fi that will, most likely, be available onboard. If such Wi-Fi is available, avoid using your mobile service if at all possible - by keeping the device in Aeroplane/Flight mode.

If you must use it, keep any calls you do need to make very short, and <u>never</u> turn on Data Roaming/Mobile Data while on a cruise ship.

7. Controlling Connectivity while Travelling

To effectively manage the use of phone, text, and data services while you travel – in particular, to avoid excess charges – it is essential to understand how to control what services are enabled and disabled.

We'll talk about the iPhone and iPad here – but same applies on non-Apple devices.

First, Aeroplane Mode

Make sure you are familiar with Aeroplane Mode on ALL your devices. It is an important setting that you will need to enable whenever you are flying – and probably at other times during your trip.

What is Aeroplane Mode?

Aeroplane mode (also known flight mode) is a setting available on smartphones and other portable devices. When activated, it turns off all signal transmission from/to your device.

This means that you won't be able to make or receive calls, send or receive text messages, or use mobile data.

While in Aeroplane Mode, you can still choose to turn on Wi-Fi and Bluetooth.

On the iPhone and iPad, Aeroplane Mode can be easily managed in the **Control Centre** or from the **Settings** app.

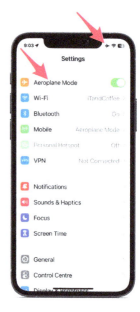

Also remember to put your Apple Watch into Aeroplane Mode.

In fact, in your Watch's Settings, it is best to choose to 'mirror' your phone's settings for Aeroplane Mode – so that enabling this mode on the iPhone ensures that the same happens on the Apple Watch.

7. Controlling Connectivity while Travelling

This is done from the **Watch** app on the iPhone, from **General -> Aeroplane Mode**

Aeroplane Mode is not just relevant to when you are flying.

It is the key setting for ensuring that your device does not incur any International Roaming charges. While your device is in this mode, no calls can be received or made, no SMSs can be sent or received, and no mobile data can be used.

If you do decide to turn off Aeroplane Mode at any point while away from your home country – perhaps just to check if any texts have been sent to you - make sure that your Data Roaming (and Mobile Data) have previously been turned off. We will look at these settings shortly.

Wi-Fi on Flights

These days, flights may offer Wi-Fi - but this service still tends to be very expensive.

Even if you do have access to Wi-Fi, you will find that download speeds and data is usually very limited – so activities like streaming of movies/entertainment is unlikely to work.

Before considering using in-flight Wi-Fi, make sure you carefully check out what is offered and the cost.

If you have multiple SIMs

If there are multiple SIMs available in your device, you have an alternative to Aeroplane mode for disabling/enabling each SIM's mobile service.

You can tap on the SIM in **Settings -> Mobile**, then disable (turn off so it is not green) the **Turn on this Line** option.

This will disable phone, SMS and mobile data for that SIM.

7. Controlling Connectivity while Travelling

Important Mobile Internet Settings

On any mobile device, there are two key settings to consider when travelling:

- **Mobile Data** – which controls whether your device tries to connect to the internet via nearby mobile phone towers using whichever SIM is currently active.
- **Data Roaming** – which controls whether your device is allowed to connect to mobile phone services offered by a network that is not your home service provider's network (but that has an arrangement with your home network provider).

When you are away from your home country, if Data Roaming is turned off, the Mobile Data setting (if turned on) will not result in mobile data usage – because your device will not be able to find any mobile towers belonging to your home network, so will not be able to make a connection.

As a rule, always leave the Data Roaming setting turned off on your device/s – and only turn it on at times when you are absolutely certain you want to use it. And leave Mobile Data turned off as well when not needed, to save battery.

Your Device's Mobile Data Settings

Settings relating to your use of mobile data are found on your iPhone in **Settings** -> **Mobile** (or **Settings** -> **Mobile Data** for iPads that have a SIM card).

If you have a single SIM card in your device, the Mobile settings will look something like shown in the image on the far right.

The switch at the top controls whether Mobile Data is enabled or disabled.

7. Controlling Connectivity while Travelling

If you have more than one SIM in your iPhone, the Mobile settings will look something like those shown in the image on the right.

In that case, the Mobile settings for each SIM must be managed individually.

And it is the first option at the top that controls which SIM is uses for Mobile Data – or if Mobile Data should be turned off. We look at these settings on the next page.

Turning off Data Roaming

If you have a single SIM,

- Go to **Mobile Data Options** (see first image below)
- Turn off **Data Roaming** (first option, as shown in second image below)
- Also consider turning on **Low Data Mode** (which limits use of mobile data by certain features and functions).
- Once you have established all these settings, turn off **Mobile Data** (which is top of the first screen in **Settings->Mobile**, as shown in first image on right).

When travelling abroad, only return here and turn on **Mobile Data** and **Data Roaming** if you are absolutely sure you mean to use it.

And certainly *never turn on Data Roaming if you are using PAYG International Roaming (unless you are prepared for the huge cost).*

7. Controlling Connectivity while Travelling

If you have multiple SIMs

In this case, you need to manage the **Mobile Data** and **Data Roaming** settings for each of the SIMs. Here's how:

- Tap on the applicable SIM in the list of **SIMs.**
- **Enable Turn on this Line** so that you can see all the mobile settings for that SIM.
- Then quickly turn off **Data Roaming** if it is turned on.
- Then disable **Turn on this Line** if you don't want to be using the SIM for any services - or leave this setting on if you do want to use phone/text for this SIM.

To choose which SIM to use for **Mobile Data** (if you have more than one SIM active) or turn off Mobile Data completely:

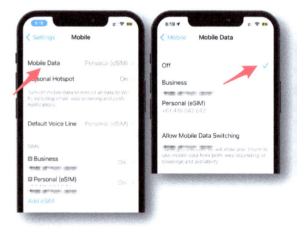

- Tap the **Mobile Data** option at the top of **Settings -> Mobile**.
- You will see the currently available SIMs (in my case here, it is one physical SIM and one eSIM)
- Choose one of these SIMs (e.g. your data-only SIM you purchased for the trip).
- Or choose **Off** if you don't want Mobile Data enabled at all (which is worth doing if you have Data Roaming off anyway, as it will save a bit of battery usage).
- If you have more than one SIM active, if you choose one of the SIMs to use for Mobile Data, also ensure that **Allow Mobile Data Switching** is turned off – so that you have full control over if and when you enable your other SIM for mobile data.

7. Controlling Connectivity while Travelling

We look further at the scenarios relating to using of multiple SIMs in Appendix D.

Network Configuration Settings

If you plug in a different SIM (pre-purchased or purchased at a destination), you may need to adjust the **Mobile Data Network** settings in order to use this SIM for mobile internet.

The instructions for the SIM should tell you the **APN settings** that need to be entered.

These details must be entered in **Settings -> Mobile**, in the **Mobile Data Network** option.

For an iPhone with any eSIMs, you must select the specific SIM from the SIMs listed in **the SIMs** section to see this option.

Then enter the APN for the SIM card into the first field.

The Username and Password fields are usually left blank.

Note that, for eSIMs installed using an app like Airalo, the APN configuration should be done for you automatically as part of the installation.

For eSIMs that you add from **Settings -> Mobile**, you may need to manually configure the APN Settings.

8. Controlling Data Usage

If you are going to be using mobile data, it is probably going to be very important to keep an eye on how much mobile data you use.

For example, if you are using your home Telco's international roaming day pass/pack, you will only have 1GB (Telstra) or 5GB (Optus). Or you may have purchased a roaming pack with a limited data allowance.

It helps to understand which apps are using your data – as well as being able to monitor your overall usage of roaming data for each day, or over a period of time.

Consider first what apps can use Mobile Data

In **Settings -> Mobile**, scroll down to see a list of Apps. (You'll need to turn on Mobile Data to see this list.)

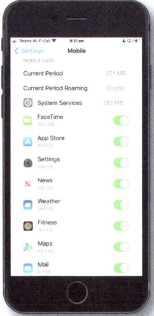

This list is showing which apps are – and are not – allowed to use mobile data (using whichever SIM is currently active). Also shown there is how much data has been used by each app (for the active SIM) since the usage statistics were last reset (which we'll talk about next).

When I travel, one of the things I do when I board the plane is to visit this area of Settings and **turn off all the apps listed here** – so that none of them are allowed to use mobile data.

Then, if I do decide to use mobile data and data roaming during my travels, I revisit this area and turn on specific apps that are allowed to use my roaming data. This prevents unexpected and unintended use of mobile data by other apps.

I would also recommend turning off 3 other settings that you will find in this area, especially for your trip - **Wi-Fi Assist**, **iCloud Drive** and **iCloud Backup** (if you see that option). These

8. Controlling Data Usage

options are towards the bottom, beneath the list of apps. All of these features can use lots of mobile data.

Monitor roaming data usage

In **Settings -> Mobile**, you can view your total Roaming Data Usage for the currently active SIM/eSIM.

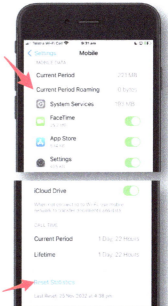

Current Period Roaming shows how much roaming data you have used since you last reset the usage statistics.

The **Current Period** figure above that shows how much data you have used in total – roaming and non-roaming.

Resetting of these usage statistics can be done at any time from this same area.

Scroll to the bottom and choose **Reset Statistics**.

If you want to track your day's data usage – in total and by app - use this feature reset the stats at the start of the 'day' relating to your pass/pack.

Just note again that the day for Telstra will be from midnight to midnight AEST, not based on a day in your current location.

Your SIM service provider's app (if there is one) will also show information about how much roaming data you have used.

As an example, on right is the information shown in the **My Telstra** app about my Day Pass, which is currently active.

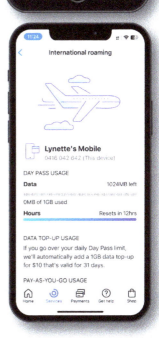

It shows the amount or data used, and how many hours until the 'day' ends (when I will incur another charge if I use any services).

8. Controlling Data Usage

If you have used an app like Airalo to purchase and install a data-only eSIM, the total roaming usage can be viewed within that app (see image on right).

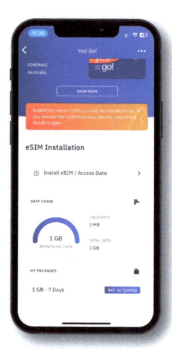

These apps are definitely very useful for monitoring the roaming data usage, and for working out when any usage period is due to end.

But I also like to use the statistics in **Settings -> Mobile**, to gain a more granular understanding of my phone's data usage by app.

This area can also be useful in advance of your trip, to gain an understanding of how much mobile data certain apps use – and how quickly they clock up this usage!

Test this out by using the app with Wi-Fi turned off and see how much usage is recorded.

Services that might use your mobile data

When you travel, it is important to consider all the things that could use internet data, whether connected to mobile data or on Wi-Fi.

Even on Wi-Fi, you may have restrictions on your data downloads/uploads, so you may want certain features turned off most of the time - and only turned on if you have suitable Wi-Fi.

A few key examples are **Background App Refresh**, **Automatic Updates** and **Backups**. Another may be **iCloud Photos**.

Background App Refresh

Background App Refresh is a feature that 'allows apps to refresh their content when on Wi-Fi or mobile data in the background'.

Turning this off can save data usage and conserve battery life – and for most apps, it does not need to be on, even when you are at home.

8. Controlling Data Usage

Visit **Settings -> General -> Background App Refresh**

You will see a list of apps and the option to turn off this service on a 'per app' basis.

Tap the first option to see your choices that can apply across all apps – to only use Background App Refresh on Wi-Fi, or to also allow it with Mobile Data.

Or choose to turn it **Off** completely, across all apps.

My approach is to turn this off for most apps, and only turn it on if I find an app does not work satisfactorily without it.

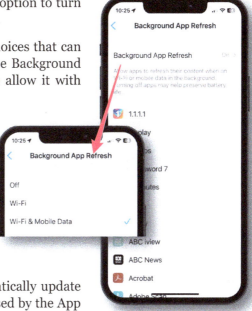

Automatic Updates

Your device may be set to automatically update Apps whenever an update is released by the App publisher.

Updates involve downloading often large files.

While you are travelling, you may choose to delay these updates until a time when you know you have a Wi-Fi capability with no restrictions.

Go to **Settings -> App Store.**

There are several settings here that can result in unexpected data usage.

Most importantly, turn off the **Mobile Data** option in the first section and further down, in the section headed MOBILE DATA, make sure **Automatic Downloads** is also turned off.

Under the heading of **AUTOMATIC DOWNLOADS** (the second section), turn off **App Downloads**, **App Updates**, **In-App Content**. Further down, turn off **Video Autoplay.**

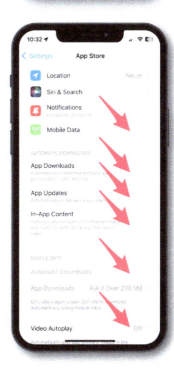

8. Controlling Data Usage

You can always manually check for any App Updates from the **App Store** app – and **UPDATE** any essentials.

To do this, tap your profile circle at top right of the **App Store** app. The number that shows on that circle represents the number of apps that need updating.

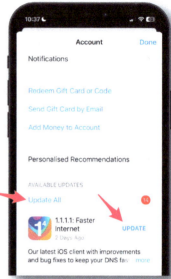

Scroll down to see a list of any **AVAILABLE UPDATES** (see image on right).

Choose to **Update All** or **UPDATE** individual apps.

iOS/iPadOS Updates

The same applies for iOS/iPadOS Software Updates. You may want to control when downloads are allowed for these updates during your trip.

Go to **Settings -> General -> Software Update -> Automatic Updates**

Turn off **Download iOS Updates**.

You may want to also turn off **Install iOS Updates** – so that you can be sure you can manually control this process at a time that suits you.

iCloud Backups

You may have set up your iPhone or iPad to automatically perform backups to iCloud. Such backups occur automatically if all of the following conditions are met:

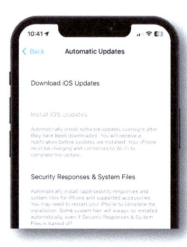

8. Controlling Data Usage

- You have enabled iCloud backups and you have sufficient space remaining in your iCloud for the backup.
- Your device is charging.
- You currently have an internet connection – usually Wi-Fi, but could be over mobile data.
- Your device is locked/asleep for long enough.
- It has been at least 24 hours since the last backup.

If you don't want backups to occur automatically, you must turn off the **Back up this iPhone** setting in **Settings -> your-name -> iCloud Backup.**

If you are happy for backups to occur over Wi-Fi, leave this setting on.

But it is strongly suggested that, especially while you travel, the **Back Up Over Mobile Data** setting is disabled.

iCloud Photos

iCloud Photos is a fantastic service that syncs your photos with your iCloud and between your Apple Devices.

If iCloud Photos is enabled (in **Settings -> your-name -> iCloud -> Photos**), photos that you take will be automatically sync'd to your iCloud when you have internet connectivity.

In **Settings -> Photos**, you can control whether that sync'ing of photos is allowed to occur over **Mobile Data.**

Tap the **Mobile Data** option in **Settings -> Photos** and then turn off **Unlimited Updates** and turn off **Mobile Data**.

Your photo sync'ing will still occur over Wi-Fi, whenever you are connected to a network.

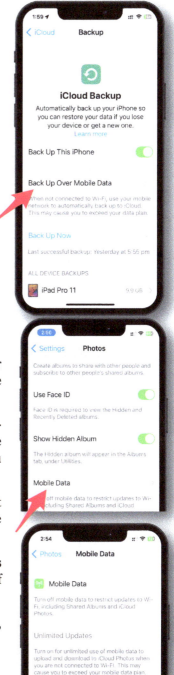

8. Controlling Data Usage

There is no easy way to fully disable sync'ing of iCloud Photos over Wi-Fi without turning off iCloud Photos completely – apart from by leaving Wi-Fi turned off.

You can, however, choose to Pause syncing of large number of photos from within the Photos App – should you need to turn on Wi-Fi for some other purpose and want to avoid photo syncing.

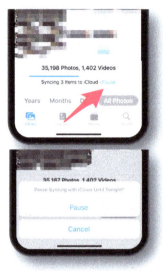

When looking at the **All Photos** or **Recents** views in Photos, you will see a sync progress bar at the very bottom – as shown in the example on the right.

Tap the word Pause to pause sync'ing of your Photos for a period. In the example on the right, the Pause is until 'tonight'.

Data use by Apple Watch

As already mentioned, it appears that the main Australian Telcos do not offer an International Roaming service for the eSIM in the Apple Watch. This means that the Apple Watch cannot work independently of the iPhone.

If your SIM provider *does* offers International Roaming for your Watch's eSIM, you can manage what apps are able to use data roaming from the **Watch** app's **Mobile** option.

As for the Mobile settings on your iPhone (and iPad), you can scroll to the bottom if the list of apps and **Reset Statistics** if you want to monitor the Watch's mobile data usage.

On the Watch itself, you can choose to turn off **Mobile Data** (or the **Mobile** service entirely) from the **Control Centre** (which is revealed by swiping up from the bottom of the screen).

8. Controlling Data Usage

The indicated symbol in the leftmost image on the previous page provides access to the **Mobile Settings**, including the list of apps that can/can't use mobile data.

Note that Aeroplane Mode can be also controlled from this Control Centre on the Watch. However, as mentioned earlier, the best plan is usually to choose to **Mirror iPhone** – so that the Watch is always in same mode as iPhone. This is done from the **Watch** app, from **General -> Aeroplane Mode**.

Then, when you need to turn on Aeroplane Mode for both your Watch and your iPhone, you can easily do this from your Watch OR your iPhone.

Do you need to consider data usage by Mail apps?

Preventing unexpected Mail downloads

If your mail is anything like mine, there can tend to be a high volume of emails that arrive each day. If you turn on your data roaming, you may not want to waste valuable data on these mail downloads – which usually happen automatically when you are connected to the internet.

Of course, you could just turn off the email app's use of mobile data, in **Settings -> Mobile** – to prevent any mail retrieval while you are away from Wi-Fi. This is certainly the easiest way to control Mail mobile data usage.

But if you are a user of the Mail app on the iPhone and iPad, you can also make a change in settings so that you can specifically choose just when the downloading of new messages should occur.

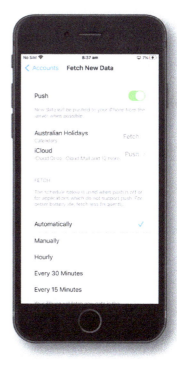

Push v Fetch v Manual in Mail

For the Mail app, settings controlling when mail is retrieved are managed from **Settings -> Mail -> Accounts -> Fetch New Data**

To conserve battery and data usage while you travel, turn off **Push** at the top.

Under that will be the list of Mail accounts that your Mail app manages, and each will show the type of retrieval that applies.

Set each account to show **Fetch** or **Manual**.

8. Controlling Data Usage

If you have set any accounts to Fetch, you can then define the 'Fetch Schedule' at the bottom, which can be Manual, every hour, every 30 mins or every 15 mins.

Automatically means that the fetch will only occur if Wi-Fi is active, and the device is being charged – a good choice for when you travel.

For any accounts set to Manual, this means that you must open the Mail App and 'pull down to refresh' the preview list of emails to request the latest emails.

Third-Party Mail apps

Note that other email apps (e.g. Gmail, Outlook) do not provide this feature.

So the best approach to avoid unexpected mobile data usage by these email apps is to turn off Mobile Data for that email app in **Settings -> Mobile -** and only turn it on if you really do need to get your mail while you are 'on the go', away from Wi-Fi.

What about other devices?

If you are taking a device other than your iPhone on your travels – one that doesn't have its own SIM – if you need that device to access the internet when you are away from Wi-Fi, you may want to give the device access to your phone's **Personal Hotspot** (see **Settings -> Personal Hotspot** on the iPhone).

It allows your iPhone to become a portable router, providing a Wi-Fi signal to other devices.

The other devices join the hotspot from their Wi-Fi settings area, thereby giving them access to the iPhone's **mobile internet connection** – using whichever SIM is currently active and connected to mobile data.

Computers tend to use a lot of internet data for all sorts of things, so you need to be very cautious about connecting to the Personal Hotspot of a device that is currently using mobile data and Data Roaming.

And your iPad could use a lot of data for various things, unless you have gone through and turned off all sorts of features (many of which are discussed earlier in this book).

8. Controlling Data Usage

Streaming of content on any device can quickly clock up big amounts of data usage.

To be safe, it is best to leave your iPhone's **Personal Hotspot** turned off unless you really have a critical need to be using it – to avoid any accidental connection and use of precious roaming data.

(Note. Not all mobile services provide such a Personal Hotspot capability. If the options in this area are greyed, and unable to be adjusted, it means that the feature is not available for the currently active SIM card.)

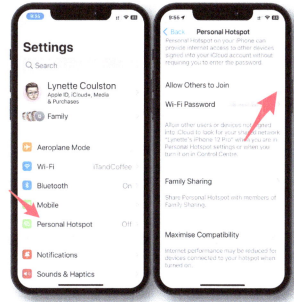

Choose your Data Mode

As mentioned on page 41, there is a Data Mode setting in **Settings-> Mobile** that controls how much mobile data is used for certain activities.

This mode saves data by reducing the quality of Facetime and other videos, turning off background processes and automatic updates (if these haven't been separately turned off), and pauses iCloud photos sync'ing.

It is found in **Settings -> Mobile -> Mobile Data Options** on iPhones with a single SIM, and in the individual SIM settings if there are multiple SIMs.

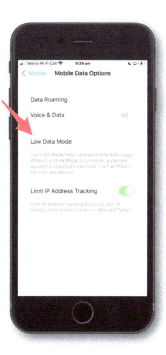

Consider using this **Low Data Mode** (or Standard Mode, if available) when you travel.

For more information about managing this setting for multiple SIMs, see Appendix D.

9. Device Preparations

Before you leave on your trip, it is important to consider some key preparations for, and considerations about, your device.

How is your Battery's health?

Make sure to check the health of your device's battery before you go.

On iPhone, go to **Settings -> Battery -> Battery Health & Charging**.

Mine is at 86% - so it often doesn't last the day. I will be considering replacing that battery before we go.

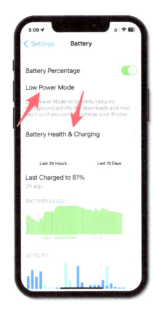

If you need to conserve battery while travelling, put your device into **Low Power Mode** in **Settings -> Battery**.

Add the **Low Power Mode** Control to your **Control Centre** to make this easy.

Hint: The list of Controls that you see in Control Centre is managed from **Settings -> Control Centre**

9. Device Preparations

As already mentioned on page 46, consider turning off **Background App Refresh** for all but essential apps as a way of conserving your battery life.

Also go to **Settings -> Privacy & Security -> Location Services** and turn off (or at least set to **While Using** or **Ask Next Time Or When I Share**) any apps that are unnecessarily using your device's location, as this can also waste the device's battery.

(Note. Don't turn off Location Services completely if you need to use it for certain apps and services – like Maps and to share your location.)

How's the device's storage?

If you are likely to take lots of photos, want to download apps, maps, translations, and more (as we will describe shortly), then you will need sufficient space on your device.

Your device's storage is fixed and can't be expanded, so before you go, it is important to check your storage.

To do this, go to **Settings -> General -> iPhone Storage** (or **iPad Storage**).

If your available storage is getting low, there are a few options for freeing up some space.

- Offload apps you don't need on the trip.
- Remove other unnecessary space hogs – see the usage data shown for each app to work out what to remove.
- Consider optimising iCloud photos to conserve space.

Let's look at each of these in a bit more detail.

'Offloading' apps that you don't need during your trip is a great option for freeing up space, as it doesn't delete the data that is associated with the app. This means you can re-download the app after the trip, and nothing is lost.

To Offload an app, tap on it in the list and choose **Offload App**. In the example on the right (Podcasts), this would free up 10.9 MB of space.

9. Device Preparations

But the real 'space hog' in this case is the actual Podcast episodes that I have downloaded to the iPhone.

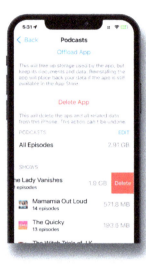

For apps like this that provide a list of downloaded/stored content, swipe right-to-left to **Delete** any content that is not required to be stored – or that you won't need during your trip.

The other suggestion shown in first image on the previous page is to conserve space by choosing to Enable the **Optimise Photos** setting (which you can also do from **Settings -> your-name -> iCloud -> Photos**).

Or, if you are not yet using iCloud Photos, you can enable that feature so that your photos can then be optimised.

This would mean smaller size versions of your photos would remain on your device, with the full resolution version stored in iCloud. This can free up a huge amount of space if you have a large Photos library.

It is certainly a good option if you are struggling to free up space otherwise.

Just a warning though: If you do decide to turn on iCloud Photos for the first time, make sure you do this well in advance of your trip so that the process of uploading and syncing your Photos library has enough time to complete before you leave. For a big library, this can take days.

Quickly accessing frequently used information

There is a feature of the iPhone that I love, and that I use every day – multiple times throughout my day, in fact. And it is so handy when you are travelling.

It is a feature called **Text Replacements**, found in **Settings -> General -> Keyboard**.

This feature allows you to set up short codes that represent longer phrases, so that typing the short code results in the full phrase replacing it.

The screen on the right shows some examples of some of my **Text Replacements.**

9. Device Preparations

While I am travelling, if I type **pp**, my passport number will appear.

If I type **emirates**, my Emirates Frequent Flyer Number will appear.

I have Text Replacements for phone numbers, my email addresses, my home address – and all sorts of other things.

If you get an OS mobile number, create a text replacement so that you don't need to keep looking up the number when you need to provide it for some form or booking. For example, set up the code OMN for that number, and only type those 3 letters to see the number magically appear.

Add a new Text Replacement by choosing the + at top right, entering the full 'Phrase' that you want to avoid typing over and over. Then, think of an easy-to-remember shortcut code for that phrase. Make sure it is not a 'real' word.

Then choose Save.

Next time you type that shortcut, the full phrase will appear on the predictive text keyboard – just tap to choose it. Or simply enter a space after the code to see the phrase replace the code.

Phone Numbers

If you do ever need to make a phone call while you are away, you will most likely need to enter an international code at the start – so you need to know how to put the + in front the country code.

For example, to call Australia, the number starts with +61.

When you are in the Keypad option of the Phone app, touch and hold your finger on the zero to get a +. Just hold your finger on that zero until the + appears.

In most cases, you will probably just use the number stored in your Contact when making calls.

So make sure that the numbers of those you will call from abroad all have the relevant international code in front of them (and are without the leading zero), especially if you are using an alternative SIM for your travel.

9. Device Preparations

Your Health Details

Something to consider before you travel – and regardless of whether you will travel – is setting up something called the **Medical ID** on your iPhone.

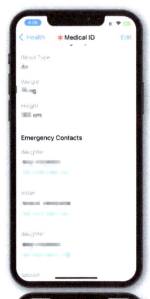

The idea of the Medical ID is that, in an emergency, the information held there could be used by emergency service and health professionals.

Your phone does not need to be unlocked in order for these professionals to access the information you have recorded there.

You can record your age, weight, height, blood type, whether you are an organ donor, plus any medical conditions and notes that might be useful.

You can also provide a list of **Emergency Contacts**.

Not only does this provide medical professionals with this important information, it also is used by the **Emergency SOS feature** of the iPhone and Apple Watch.

This feature can be activated manually on the iPhone in an emergency (where the method of activation is defined in **Settings -> Emergency SOS**) or automatically if you have an **Apple Watch** with **Fall Detection** or **Crash Detection**.

To create and update this **Medical ID**, go to **Settings -> Health - > Medical ID**.

Or you can access **Medical ID** option from within the **Health** App, by tapping the profile circle at top right when viewing the **Summary** option at bottom.

9. Device Preparations

Get your device up to date

We will talk later (in chapter 19.) about your security when travelling – and one of the most important preparations in terms of ensuring the security of your device is to make sure that you have installed the latest version of the operating system.

Each time there is an update, there is usually a range of security patches that plug potential security holes for our devices.

To see if there is an update available for your device, visit **Settings -> General-> Software Update**.

It is always recommended that you have a recent backup before applying any update – just in case anything goes wrong during the update.

It is also worth checking that all your apps are up to date

To do this, tap your profile circle at top right of the **App Store** app.

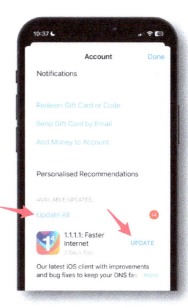

Scroll down to see a list of any **AVAILABLE UPDATES**.

Choose to **Update All** or **UPDATE** individual apps as required.

10. Let's Talk Messaging - Messages

The **Messages** app on the iPhone and iPad can be, at times, be very confusing.

And it is when you are travelling that things can get even more confusing.

While we are not going to attempt to provide a full guide to Messages as part of this book, let's talk about what it does, and why you might (or might not) want to use it when you travel.

Green vs Blue

First, it is very important to understand the message colours in the Messages app of iPad and iPhone.

- Green = **SMS** – which uses phone/text allowance (i.e. using the SIM card).
- Blue = **iMessage** – message sent via the internet (using either Wi-Fi or mobile data), to another Apple/iMessage user.

10. Let's Talk Messaging - Messages

How do I know which applies when I send?

While it is may be obvious from previous messages you have sent that you normally use Blue (iMessage) or Green (SMS) to message a particular contact, before you start a new message, you can check what your next message will be from the words in the message box at the bottom – the box in which you type your message.

If it says **iMessage** (as in the left-most image above), you will be using Wi-Fi or mobile data and sending the message via the internet. Otherwise, it will show **Text Message** if the message will be sent as an SMS.

iMessage only works if the other person is also an Apple user, you have both turned on iMessage in **Settings->Messages,** and you are both currently connected to the internet on at least one of your devices.

If there is no internet connection available for you or the other person when you send the message, it will most likely send as an SMS (or not send at all).

Just a note that, if your device is connected to Wi-Fi, but that Wi-Fi network does not currently have an internet connection, the message won't send as an iMessage – and you will have to option to send it as an SMS instead.

iMessage using Apple ID

When you turn on the iMessage feature of an iPhone, the mobile number associated with your SIM card is registered for iMessage. This means that, when you send a message to another iMessage user, your iMessage shows up as coming from your phone number (and shows as blue on your own device).

10. Let's Talk Messaging - Messages

If the recipient of the message is not an iMessage user, the message will instead go as an SMS from your phone number.

You also have the choice of signing-in to your Apple ID (iCloud account) for iMessage. The advantage of this is that your other devices (like the iPad and Mac) can then sign in to iMessage and see the same iMessages – as well as also send iMessages that appear to come from your iPhone.

If the phone's iMessage is not signed into your Apple ID, only the phone can see and send these messages.

The other advantage of signing in to iMessage with your Apple ID is that, if your SIM card is removed or deactivated – something you may choose to do when you travel - you can still send iMessages (internet messages) using your Apple ID instead of your phone number.

The difference will be that, for the recipient of your message, the 'from' will be your Apple ID (and email address) instead of the usual mobile number.

If the recipient has your email address recorded against your Contact Card (in their Contacts app), the message will still show up as coming from you.

But if your email address is not recorded in their Contacts, the message will show your email address as the sender – which may cause a bit of confusion.

If you are not using your usual SIM or have removed/deactivated your usual SIM, make sure you let the recipients know who you are when you send a message from abroad – just in case your Apple ID is not in their Contacts.

Note that you can sign in to iMessages on an iPad or Mac using your Apple ID, thereby allowing those devices to send iMessages. However, if your iPhone is not also signed in to your Apple ID, the messages on the iPad/Mac will not match those on the iPhone.

Confused yet?

If you are using a different SIM while travelling

If you insert different SIM in your iPhone (or activate a new SIM that is not your usual eSIM), that SIM may activate for iMessage as well.

10. Let's Talk Messaging - Messages

When you send an SMS or an iMessage, that alternative SIM's phone number will appear as an unknown sender for the recipient.

So, again, make sure to include mention of who you are in the message and explain why the number is different.

Although be aware that you still might look like a scammer and need to provide some evidence that you are legitimate, as there are currently active scams involving fake 'Hi Mum' messages! If you haven't heard of this scam, just Google 'Hi Mum scams' for more information.

How do I determine what 'From' will appear for others

You can see and control the 'from' phone number or Apple ID for your iMessages, in **Settings -> Messages -> Send and Receive**.

It is in the bottom section **START NEW CONVERSATIONS FROM** that you choose the 'from' phone number or email address that should apply to iMessages you send.

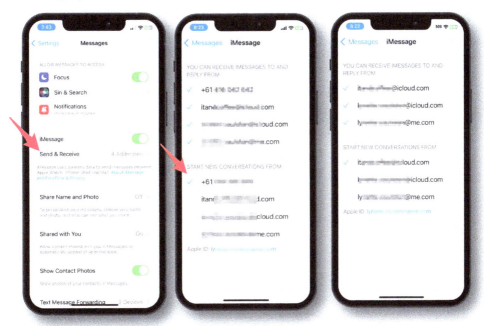

If your usual SIM has been removed or deactivated, you will not see its number in this list – as shown in the above example on the far right.

Instead, the tick will be against your Apple ID – assuming no other SIM is currently active (something we cover on page 65). Note that I have extra email addresses showing in the above example due to some Aliases I have set up for my Apple ID. Normally, you will just see one or two email addresses here – your Apple ID and any Apple email address you have set up.

If the tick is against the wrong item, just tap to tick the correct one.

If you have multiple devices using Messages

I know that this whole iMessage vs SMS concept is confusing and complicated, and it gets even more so when you travel.

If you have more than one Apple device connected to the internet (perhaps an iPad that you have left turned on at your accommodation), you may encounter an issue with SMS vs iMessage as you are 'on the go' during the day.

It is important to be aware of this issue. Let me explain the scenario where this happened on my own travels.

My husband and I were travelling abroad without our children, and I needed to send an urgent SMS to my eldest child (using my home SIM/number).

Because I had my Mobile Data and Data Roaming turned off, I turn off Aeroplane Mode to send my message as an SMS (which, in this case, would incur a PAYG charge – as I didn't have a 'day pass' turned on for that trip). I asked for a fast reply from my child – which, frustratingly, didn't come.

A couple of further SMS's to that person failed to generate a response during that day – until we connected to Wi-Fi at the end of the day, when all the replies from my child suddenly flooded in. They were iMessages, not SMSs. She had replied quickly as requested.

The reason I didn't receive the replies as SMSs on my iPhone was that I had left my iPad on (in 'sleep' mode) and connected to Wi-Fi in the hotel room – and it was therefore receiving the responses from my child (who was using an iPhone) as iMessages.

If a message can be sent over iMessage, this will be the preferred format to SMS. So you need to be aware of whether the recipient of your message is an iMessage user, and whether you have any devices currently connected to iMessage.

If I am not using Data Roaming and I want to ensure that I receive any message sent from an Apple/iMessage user as an SMS (instead of an iMessage), I need

10. Let's Talk Messaging - Messages

to ensure that there is no other device (other than my iPhone) currently connected to iMessage.

I should have turned off that iPad while I was out for the day, or just turned off iMessage on that device.

If you have two SIMs/phone numbers currently active

If you have two active phone numbers from which you can send a Message (i.e. you have two SIMs currently active in **Settings -> Mobile**), the choice can be made about which phone number/SIM to use when sending your Message.

The screen on right shows my current setup in **Settings -> Messages -> Send and Receive**, where both phone numbers are ticked in the top section – which means both can be used for sending and receiving iMessages. I could choose to 'untick' either of those numbers if I don't want to use iMessage (internet messaging) for that number – in which case, any message sent/received using that number would be a Text Message (SMS).

Choose ⬜ to start a new Message.

Enter recipient/s for the message in the **To:** field.

You will then see the **From:** field under that - showing the default number/SIM that will apply for the message.

Tap **From:** to choose to use the alternative number.

If the selected number is not enabled for iMessage, the Message will send as an SMS (Text Message).

If the number IS enabled for iMessage AND there is available internet (mobile or Wi-Fi), the Message will send as an iMessage IF the recipient is an iMessage user – otherwise it will send as an SMS.

Always look in the message bar (where you type your message text) to see how the message will be sent.

For more details on managing multiple SIMS, see Appendix D.

11. Let's Talk Messaging – Other Apps

As already mentioned earlier, it is possible to get through most of your trip without needing any phone and SMS service – by using Apps for messaging, audio calls and video calls.

These apps use mobile data or Wi-Fi instead of the phone/SMS service.

Let's look first at the topic of Messaging using other apps.

Most Popular options

WhatsApp, **Facebook Messenger,** and **Telegram** are three of the most popular messaging apps. Some other options are Viber, Instagram Messenger, Snapchat, and Skype.

The key thing to note when using such apps is that both ends of the conversation must be using the same App - so, you may need to use different apps for messaging different people in your life, depending on which app they choose to use.

Let's look at a couple of the most popular options.

Facebook Messenger

Messenger requires you to have a Facebook account to set it up. We use it extensively for family group chats – and it works very well.

If you don't want to use Facebook, you can deactivate the Facebook aspect after setting up Messenger and still use Messenger.

11. Let's Talk Messaging – Other Apps

Download the Messenger App from Apple's App Store.

Start a new conversation with an individual or a group from the **Chats** area of the app (icon at bottom left, as indicated in previous image), and use the 'compose' symbol at top right to create a new chat. You will then choose who you wish to message – and this must be someone who is already a Facebook user.

Alternatively, tap on a 'conversation' in the list of chats that appear and send a message to the person/group that way. The name or names of those associated with the conversation are shown in that preview list.

We won't go further into how to use the Messenger app here but do make sure to try it out before you go - if that is the app (or just one of the apps) that you will use.

WhatsApp

WhatsApp is one of the most popular messaging apps.

With WhatsApp, you register an account using your mobile number.

People can then message you via WhatsApp using your mobile number.
Even though your mobile number is used, the message is not an SMS – it is an internet message.

Many businesses will support communications via WhatsApp.

Again, make sure you set up the App (download it from the App Store) before you go abroad.

As for Messages and Messenger, a list of previous conversations is shown when you tap the Chats option at the bottom. Tap any item in the list to continue the conversation with the person or group.

Or use the Compose symbol at the top right to send a message to someone (or a group) that you don't see in the list.

Make sure to give WhatsApp access to your Contacts. Otherwise, you will need to manually set up your WhatsApp Contacts.

11. Let's Talk Messaging – Other Apps

Those Contacts who are users of WhatsApp will appear in the New Chat list with a message underneath their name. If there is no such message, that person is not currently a WhatsApp user – because their phone number is not associated with a WhatsApp account.

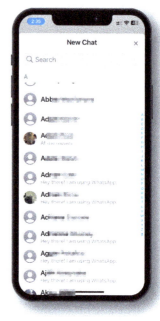

So you can't message or call them using WhatsApp.

One thing to consider in relation to WhatsApp when travelling – what happens if you take out your usual SIM, so your normal phone number is no longer available? Will WhatsApp still work?

WhatsApp will continue to work even if you take out or turn off your home SIM, because it is an internet messaging app that does not actually use your phone service. The only problem you might incur is if you need to re-verify your account, which requires that you can receive an SMS to your usual number.

This is another good reason to make sure you travel with your home SIM, even if you don't plan to use it.

Here's what is stated on the WhatsApp website in relation to travelling and using an alternative SIM (or removing of the usual SIM).

> When you are traveling out of the country, you can still use WhatsApp account via mobile data or Wi-Fi.
>
> If you use a local SIM card while you are traveling, you can still use WhatsApp with your home number. However in this case, if you need to re-verify your account, you won't be able to do this while using the local SIM card. To re-verify / verify a phone number with WhatsApp, you must have the corresponding SIM card in your phone, with phone or SMS service enabled.

Make sure to test before you go

Whatever app/s you are going to use while travelling, make sure they work before you go.

Set up 'group chats' for the people with whom you wish to communicate as a group.

Start a conversation within the app/s with important contacts and groups, so that you can be sure both ends of the 'tunnel' are open and working.

12. Calling Options via Apps

Audio only or Audio and Video Calls

As for messaging, you don't need to have a phone service to be able to make and receive calls. The messaging apps mentioned above all have audio and video chat capabilities – allowing you to talk one-on-one or have group audio or video calls over the internet.

Audio calls use much less internet than video calls – but try to avoid either of these when using mobile data and roaming.

As with messaging, you need both parties in the call to be able to use the same service. Tap the **Calls** option at the bottom, then the 'New Call' symbol at top right. Then search for the applicable contact and choose the symbol to make an audio call or for a video call.

Below are examples of WhatsApp (left) and Messenger (right) call options and screens.

12. Calling Options via Apps

Use Facetime for Apple to Apple

If you need to make an audio or video call to another Apple user, Apple's **Facetime** app is your best and the easiest option.

Just ask **Siri** to *Facetime Audio Call Jo Bloggs*

Or say *Facetime Jo Bloggs* for a video call.

If you don't want to use Siri, you can also open the FaceTime app and start a **New FaceTime** from within the App (see screen on right).

Or you can look up person in the **Contacts** app and choose the Facetime Audio or Video Call option (as shown in the image below).

Just look for the **Facetime** section, found under the 'phone' section in the Contact card (as shown below).

Remember though – for you to be able call them using Facetime, the other person must be an Apple user who has enabled Facetime – so test this out before you go on your trip.

And if you want to avoid accidentally using mobile data for making FaceTime calls, go to **Settings -> Mobile** and make sure you turn off Facetime there.

13. Let's Talk Flights

In the next couple of chapters, we will talk about flights and accommodation. We will not try to give an extensive coverage of either of these topics, but rather will offer some suggestions for websites and apps that are worthy of consideration.

Google Flights

Google Flights is a handy tool that allows you to explore flights, see prices across various providers, use filters to help with selection of your flights, and then track prices over a period of time.

You can look up one-way, return, or multi-city flights.

In fact, the site www.google.com/travel offers lots of other travel-related curation topics – hotels, holiday rentals, train tickets, things to do, and more.

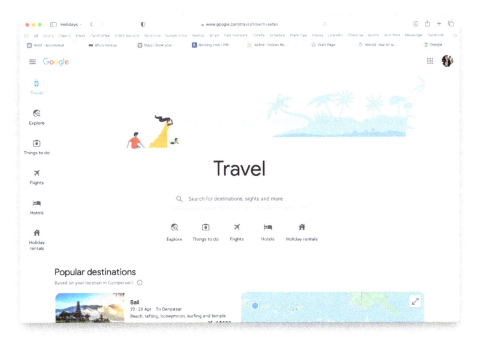

For the flights option, when you pop in your destination and click on the departure date field, you will see calendar of dates and prices – allowing you to see which departure and return dates offers the cheapest flights. (See next page for examples.)

13. Let's Talk Flights

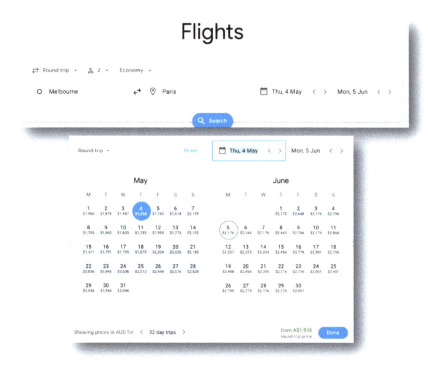

When you Search, you will be presented with a list of 'departing flight' options – and can then choose the sort order for these options, looking for the cheapest first, or perhaps the flights with the shortest flying time.

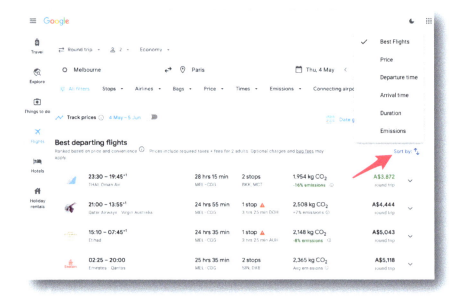

13. Let's Talk Flights

When you choose one of the flights from the list shown, you will then be asked to choose your return flight (assuming you have chosen that option). If it is a multi-leg flight, you will then choose the next leg from the options provided.

Once you have made your selections, you will be presented with the some booking options with different providers. I tend to leave Google here and look for the same flight on alternative sites. But it is handy for getting started.

I also use Google Flights to track flight prices over time, especially when I am booking well in advance and want to get a sense of when to book. For that, I turn on the **Track prices** switch for the chosen flight/s (indicated with the arrow below). (Note. I must be signed in with a Google account to do this.)

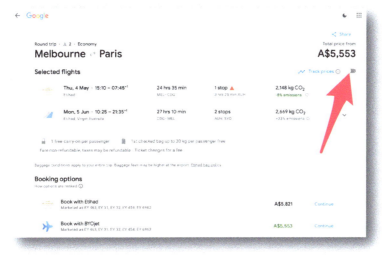

I can then monitor my tracked flights at www.google.com/travel/flights/saves.

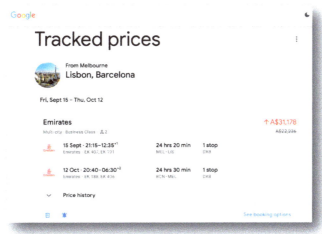

13. Let's Talk Flights

The **Price History** option shows a graph like that below. Hover your mouse over the graph to see the actual price that applied on past dates.

Other options

Of course, there are lots of other options for finding and booking flights online – and for tracking prices.

Some sites are 'online travel agents' – allowing you to make and manage your bookings via these sites.

These are sites such as Booking.com, Webjet, Flight Centre, and Expedia.

Others are 'aggregator' sites, curating options from other sites and presenting you with a list of option.

Examples of aggregator sites are Skyscanner, Travelocity, TripAdvisor., Cheapflights, KAYAK, Momondo.

While you may have heard reports that you should always browse these sites in 'incognito/private' mode (so that the history of what you search is not tracked and used to elevate prices when you come back to a flight), this is apparently not necessary.

Prices shown are based on demand and various other things – not your browsing history.

It is well worth comparing prices across these different sites – to check that you have the best deal, taking care to consider if you are comparing like for like.

13. Let's Talk Flights

Comparing flight options

Site Qualities	Booking.com	KAYAK	Webjet
Best	Best Overall	Best for Flexibility	Australian Owned
Price	Best	Average	Average
Flexibility	+/- 3 days	+/- 3 days	+/- 3 days
Comparison Tools	Average	Best	Average
Usability	Best	Average	Average

Here are two articles comparing online travel agent websites:

- www.flyparks.com.au/blog/best-flight-search-sites
- www.thriftynomads.com/booking-cheapest-flight-possible-anywhere

It is always important to compare 'apples with apples', and make sure you are aware of inclusions/exclusions/fees/etc.

- Beware of any servicing fee from the website (on top of the price shown).
- Is baggage included? What is the baggage allowance? Are there extra fees?
- Consider the option of booking direct with the Airline once you work out the best fare.
- Or visit a travel agent armed with the information you have researched.

Before your fly

Make sure you check with your airline if there are any restrictions on devices and other things in your carry-on and checked-in luggage.

In particular, think about any portable batteries you are carrying – are they allowed in the cabin?

During flight

Many flights these days will offer USB charging ports. So make sure to have your charging cable and any adaptor you need for the flight.

On planes or in any other public place, beware of charging ports that give a prompt on your device asking you to 'trust' them.

13. Let's Talk Flights

Never say yes to this question if it appears on your screen for any public USB charging port you use - as it is asking for access to data on your device.

There have been recent reports that, in some public places, USB charging ports can be quite dangerous, with the potential that there may be hackers using them to infect attached devices with malware and other software.

While perhaps not such an issue on planes (and hopefully very rare elsewhere) just be aware of this concern whenever you are away from home.

I prefer to charge only portable chargers using such USB charging ports – and then use the portable charger to charge my device.

If there is the offer of a power point, this should be used in preference to a USB port – but you will, of course, need to make sure to have the relevant international adaptor for such a power point.

If you don't have any charging facility on your flight, make sure you are aware of how to conserve your battery during long flights. Perhaps consider keeping your device in **Low Power Mode** or turned off. We covered some other battery considerations on page 54.

Your Tickets and Boarding Passes

Put your boarding passes into Apple Wallet (if offered as an option).

Make sure you get the App (or Apps) associated with any airline you will be travelling with.

But don't just rely on website or app access for your travel documentation.

Make sure you have versions that are stored on your device, and don't need internet to access them.

A recent Ticketek meltdown at a Melbourne concert proved what can happen if you need internet or app access, and if that service is not available at the time you need access to your ticket.

13. Let's Talk Flights

In that example, those without proof of tickets had to queue up for manual tickets, instead of being easily admitted using their e-ticket.

I always save any tickets and boarding passes as PDFs – for example, in Files or Notes. (We'll talk about all your travel documents in chapter 15.) I also use TripIt (described from page 89) for all tickets and other trip documentation.

14. Let's Talk Accommodation

Book Hotel Accommodation Online

As with flights, there is a large range of websites available for exploring and booking your hotel accommodation. Many travellers use this option to organise their trip – rather than engaging a travel agent.

The price of the accommodation will be pretty much the same across the board but do always check the cancellation/changes policy for the room/accommodation that you are considering.

As for flights, some websites are 'online travel agencies' – for example, Booking.com, Expedia.com, Wotif.com, Hotels.com, Agoda.com

There are also other sites that are 'aggregator' sites - that show a range of options and provide links to jump to the selected site to book.

Some examples of aggregator sites are Google Travel, Trivago.com, Tripadvisor.com, and Kayak.com.

Here's a Choice article that is worth a read, in relation to booking hotels online: www.choice.com.au/travel/accommodation/hotels/buying-guides/hotel-booking

Book Other Accommodation

When you are looking at Accommodation, there are lots of options other than hotels. You can book rooms, apartments, and entire homes.

Here's an article that provides a review of options for short-term rentals: www.smartertravel.com/best-vacation-rental-sites-short-term-rental/

14. Let's Talk Accommodation

Which ones did I use?

We have just booked all our accommodation for a trip later this year, all done online using a variety of online sites.

We used Booking.com, Airbnb, Expedia, and VRBO (which used to be HomeAway), and our bookings are for combination of hotels and apartments.

In a couple of locations we have booked accommodation with friends, so needed a place that would accommodate 6 people. These were booked using VRBO.

Just be careful when reviewing the options presented, as you will find that the cheapest option usually doesn't allow cancellations. If you pay a bit more, you will usually have the option to cancel up until closer to the date.

I did find that, for several searches, the options presented by Expedia didn't seem to offer cancellations.

If I liked the look of the place that I found on Expedia, I then looked it up on Booking.com – and found an option that did allow cancellation/changes.

For many bookings, you may be able to pay later – but will usually need to provide credit card details at the time of booking.

14. Let's Talk Accommodation

Take advantage of the provided maps

I did like Expedia better for the maps it provided of accommodation, as it showed the indicative price for each place on the map view.

On right is such a map from Expedia.

Clicking on any of the options shown provides more information at the bottom.

With the Booking.com map shown below, you must hover the mouse over (or tap) to see more details of each place marker.

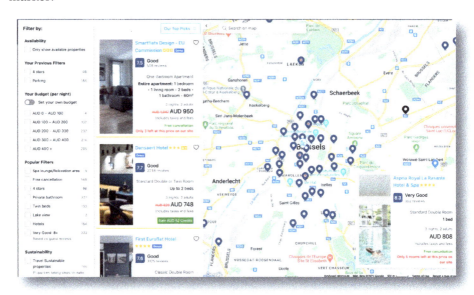

Using these maps, we would look at what we wanted to stay near (e.g. stations, city square, some attraction), then see what options were available near that/those places.

The prices on the map helped us focus on the options that were within our budget.

14. Let's Talk Accommodation

Confirmations/Communications

When you book through any of these online sites, confirmation information is provided via email – so make sure to file your emails for later reference (and check your Junk Mail if you don't see such a confirmation).

Of course, this means it is important to get your email address right whenever you book something online. You will normally need to create an account using your email address.

We'll talk shortly about options for digitally storing the information about your accommodation and other aspects of your itinerary – including a particular app that does a fantastic job of collating and presenting your itinerary.

Make sure also to get the app associated with each booking site you have used – as these apps will show all your bookings and all the information you require about those bookings.

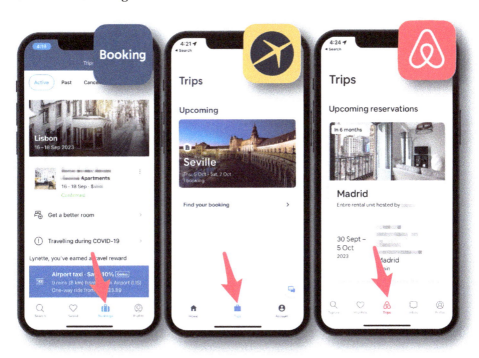

15. Your travel documentation

If you are booking a lot of your trip on your own – or even if you use a travel agent – there will inevitably be heap of documentation related to your trip.

So let's look at some options for ensuring that this documentation is available to you when you need it – without needing to take wads of paperwork!

Get documentation into digital format

It is well worth collating all the travel documentation as you prepare for your trip and getting it into digital format – even if you do end up taking some (or all) of it in paper format.

Use your iPhone (or iPad) to scan physical documents into electronic format. Each can be saved to Files or Notes. You don't need a scanner to do this. The Files and Notes apps both provide a **Scan** function.

Scan your passport and store it securely. This can be in a Locked Note, as long as the scan is a photo or series of photos (not a PDF).

15. Your travel documentation

Cloud services like OneDrive and Dropbox also allow you to scan and store documents. My OneDrive has a Personal Vault for securely storing sensitive documents.

If you do choose to store your files in a cloud storage service – whether that be iCloud Drive (through Files), OneDrive, Dropbox, or Google Drive, make sure these files are available 'offline' - i.e. that they are stored on your device instead of 'on demand', so that they don't need internet to access them.

In the example on the right – showing a folder in my **Files** app - there are two files that are not stored on my device, indicated by the cloud symbol on the right side.

To ensure they are stored and available even if I don't have internet, I need to touch and hold on the item and choose **Download Now**.

In OneDrive, I must tap the **...** symbol and choose **Make Available Offline**.

We won't go further into the topic of scanning and storing files on your mobile device, as this is a whole separate topic (and class that iTandCoffee runs regularly, also available on video).

Contact iTandCoffee if you need to learn more about these topics, as we have various videos covering these topics.

Use Apple's Notes for all sorts of travel info

Another great option – which I am utilising extensively for our next trip – is Apple's **Notes** app.

Apple Notes can store all sorts of information in a single Note, so offers a great solution for collating all the information about each part of your trip.

In the Notes app, create a folder/sub-folder structure for storing your travel Notes.

Make sure that this folder is stored in iCloud – so that it syncs to other devices and is available from iCloud.com - should something happen to your device.

Each Note can contain pictures, website links, PDFs, text, to-do's - anything!

15. Your travel documentation

And, as mentioned above, Notes provides a scan option to scan straight into Notes.

Notes is also great for curating articles and web pages that relate to the trip – things to do, accommodation that looks good, and so much more.

By 'sharing' 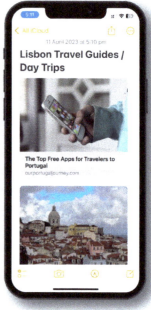 the web page from Safari to a Note, you get a 'friendly' link that shows a photo and the topic of the link, making your curated links a lot more visual. See an example on the right.

Name your Notes for easy sorting and locating and consider using Tags to further classify them.

The screen shot of my iPad below shows the list of Notes I have created (so far) in a folder for our upcoming trip.

I have named the Notes so that 'like' notes are grouped together when I sort the Notes alphabetically.

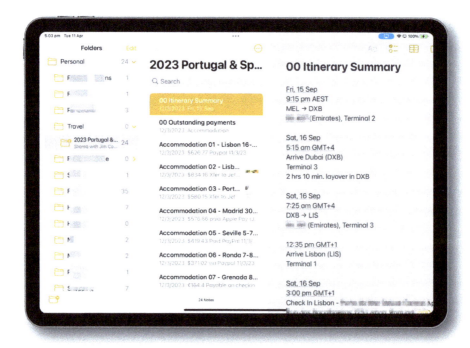

15. Your travel documentation

For the emails that I received that confirmed accommodation, flights, transport, tours, etc, I created a PDF of each email and added it to a Note that collected all the information about that part of the trip. Any attachment in the email has also been saved to that same Note separately (as the content of these attached PDF will not be included in the PDF version of the mail message).

As an example, for each accommodation Note, I have the PDF of the email, a photo of the accommodation (to jog my memory of what we booked), pasted details like dates, phone number, address, booking reference number, check-in time, the Maps reference, a screenshot of the map, plus anything else that might be useful once we get there.

This means that everything is available in one place, and I don't need internet to access it.

Creating a PDF from Mail Messages

You may have noticed that the Mail app on the iPhone and iPad does not seem to provide the option to create a PDF from a Mail message. So you may be wondering how I created PDFs from the confirmation/booking emails.

Most of the time, I use my Mac computer to do this. I can easily save any email as a PDF from there – from the **File** menu, using the **Export as PDF** option.

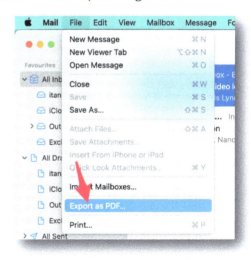

And, on the Mac, the Print option also provides the option to save the 'print' as a PDF instead of physically printing it.

But it's really handy to know that there is a way to create PDFs from the Mail app on the iPad and iPhone for the times you need to do this.

In fact, the same applies to any other app on the iPhone/iPad that has a Print option.

Here are the steps to generate a PDF from a Mail message – which involves 'printing' the message but not actually sending it to the printer.

- Open the Mail message with the confirmation details.
- Choose ↩ then the **Print option.**

15. Your travel documentation

- The Print screen includes a preview of the document.
- Put two fingers on this preview and pinch outwards – like when you Zoom inwards on something on the screen.
- You will be presented with the 'print' formatted version of your email – which is actually a PDF.
- Choose the Share symbol
- Choose where to save this PDF – e.g. tap **Notes** to add the PDF to a Note, choose **Save to Files** to save the PDF as a file in iCloud Drive (found then in the Files app), or perhaps choose an alternative cloud storage service like OneDrive, Google Drive, or Dropbox.

Share your Notes Folder

A relatively new feature of the Notes app is the ability to share a Notes folder with another Apple iCloud user.

The screen on the right appears when the Share symbol in chosen at top right, when viewing a Notes folder.

Choose to Share the folder as 'view-only' (where those sharing cannot make changes) or in a way that allows those sharing to make updates to (Edit) the content of the folder.

Then, choose the person or people who will share the folder.

The easiest way to do this is using Messages.

To see and manage the people who share the folder, tap the circle at the top that shows the other face/s, then **Manage Shared Folder** or **Show Folder Activity.**

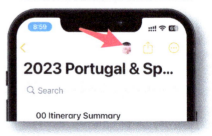

We'll leave that topic there. But if you need more information about the Notes app, iTandCoffee has videos of classes on this topic.

15. Your travel documentation

Don't forget to take those passwords

Make sure you travel with your passwords!

The best approach for managing passwords is to use a Password Safe – and there are several well-known, excellent apps that provide such a capability. Examples are 1Password, LastPass and Dashlane.

In fact, your iPad, iPhone and Mac has a built-in password manager called Keychain – used by Safari to auto-fill login creditials for online sites. (Note that Keychain is protected by your device's passcode/password, so should only be used in you use a strong passcode/password.)

Another option to consider is using a locked Note (or multiple locked Notes) in the Notes app for storing these passwords. This will then give you access to that information when you are 'on the go'.

I know many readers will have physical notebooks of passwords, or a page of passwords – or even store passwords in the Contacts app. It is not a great idea to rely on solutions like this for your travels (or at any time). From a security perspective is certainly a risky approach to travel with such a notebook/paper list.

Consider scanning each page of passwords into a Note (as images), then choose to **Lock Note**.

Such locked Notes can be unlocked using Touch or Face ID or using the passcode that has been established for locked Notes.

Lock Other Confidential Notes

For security, make sure you lock any other Notes that contain anything that should be protected.

Notes that have PDFs or Tags cannot be locked – but other Notes can.

If you do want to lock something that you scan into Notes, you will need to make sure that it is scanned as an image, not a PDF. If you want to learn more about Locking of Notes, iTandCoffee has a video that looks at the Notes app in detail.

15. Your travel documentation

Save the Dates

The **Mail** app of the iPad and iPhone offers a handy feature that will appear whenever there is event and date information in an email.

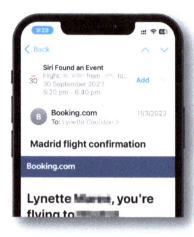

You can see at the top of the email in the screen image on the right are the words **Siri Found an Event**.

By tapping **Add** if you see such a message, a draft event then appears (see below left) – and you can simply tap Add to add the event to your Calendar.

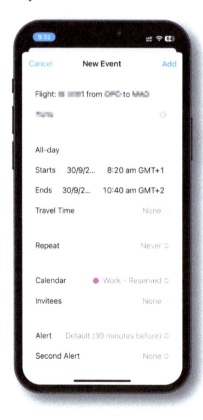

15. Your travel documentation

Your Itinerary in an App - Tripit

An excellent option for collecting all sorts of information about your itinerary is the **Tripit** app.

Any email you receive about flights, accommodation, transport, day trips, car rentals, and more can be forwarded to **Tripit** - and your itinerary is magically updated to reflect information that has been extracted from that email and any attachment it had.

Your forwarded email must be sent to Tripit from the email account that you registered when setting up the Tripit app and you forward the email to the address **plans@tripit.com.**

At the Tripit end, the received email is matched to a Tripit account based on that 'from' email address, and the information in the email is extracted and added to the trip itinerary.

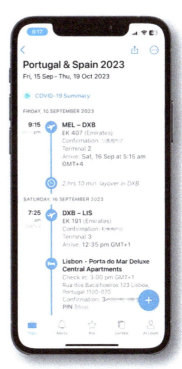

The screen shot on the right shows an example of the itinerary for a trip we have planned. If I tap on any of the items in the itinerary, further information is available.

For flights, it provides departure and arrival times, confirmation code, terminal numbers, seat numbers, whether check-in is available yet and more.

I can view the itinerary from Tripit.com – as well as from the Tripit App.

A detailed or summarised itinerary can be printed or generated as a PDF.

15. Your travel documentation

You can securely add travel documents to Tripit, get personalised alerts relating to safety, track your travel stats and more.

Activities, bookings etc. can be manually added as well.

I will produce summarised and detailed output of our Tripit itinerary before we go and add these to my Notes, in my Travel folder.

This is so that I have all the information in a format that doesn't have to rely on Tripit (just in case there is any issue accessing the app while travelling).

You may have guessed that I like to have backup plans for all the documentation!

Tripit provides the ability to add your itinerary to your Calendar, as a 'subscribed' calendar – and makes it very easy to do this.

Simply tap **Account** (option on the bottom right of the app) and **Settings** option, and choose the **Calendar Sync** option, then the **Add Tripit to Your Apple Calendar.**

You will then see an option to **Subscribe.**

Once you select that option, you will be able to review the subscribed calendar – and choose the Calendar account and colour.

(We won't go into this in more detail here. You can just choose to accept whatever defaults appear, to keep things simple.)

Choose **Add** at top right to add the calendar to your Calendar app.

Then take a look at your Calendar app – to see all the events that Tripit has added for each of the items in your itinerary.

15. Your travel documentation

Tripit also provides other features if you pay for the Pro version, which is $77.99 per year.

- ☐ Get real-time alerts on flight departures / delays
- ☐ Get up to date terminal and gate info
- ☐ A currency converter
- ☐ Info on Tipping customs
- ☐ Embassy information
- ☐ Language and time zone information
- ☐ Socket and plug requirements
- ☐ Required vaccinations
- ☐ Communication information
- ☐ Driving advice

Of course, there are other apps that do similar things to Tripit. Here is an article that talks about some of these:
https://www.travelinglifestyle.net/best-travel-planning-apps

Your Travel To-Dos

I maintain a **Notes** 'tick list' of items I need to pack and things I need to remember to do, and make sure I update this list as soon as I think of things.

The **Reminders** app is also important in our preparations – allowing the setup of 'to dos' that have date and time alerts associated with them, so that I get a notification about the Reminder item on a particular day and at a nominated time.

As an example, we can't book some of our train tickets until about 3 months prior to the trip – so I have set Reminders for relevant dates.

I also have Reminders to register our trip with the bank, activate our travel insurance, and more.

16. Speaking the language

Discovering Translation Apps

If you are going to a country where English is not the primary language, it is important to consider how you will communicate – and Translation apps offer a great solution.

Apple's Translate App

There is a standard Apple translation app on the iPhone and iPad – called **Translate**.

If you don't see it in your list of available apps, it can be downloaded for no cost from Apple's App Store.

The Translate app allows for pre-downloading of languages for as many countries as needed (assuming you have available storage on your device) – so that can then do translations at a time when you don't have internet.

To pre-download one or more translation files, visit **Settings -> Translate -> Downloaded Languages**

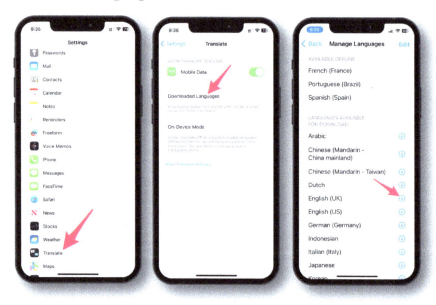

Make sure to download English as well as other languages that are required during your trip. Your offline translations won't work without the English

16. Speaking the language

download. And make sure you have enough storage space for any languages that you want to store.

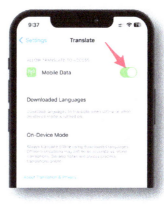

You can also choose to disable the use of Mobile Data by the Translate app – and just rely on the downloaded languages while you are away from Wi-Fi.

If you want the Translate app to only use the downloaded languages (even if Wi-Fi is available), turn on the **On Device Mode**. (I will leave this setting turned off, as the translations may not be as good.)

In the Translation app, select the 'from' and 'to' languages at the top. You will see a message if you are not connected to the internet and the selected language has not yet been downloaded (as shown in left-most image below).

Using the **Translate** option at bottom left, tap 🎤 to speak, or just tap to type something in English in the space where you see **Enter text.** You will then see the translation in the chosen language.

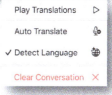

The **Conversation** option at the bottom is useful when talking to a person who does not speak your language. Tap the circled ... to see options to choose to 'auto-

16. Speaking the language

detect' the language of each party, to listen and automatically translate conversation, and to play audio of the translations (as well as showing text on the screen).

Select ⬚ to split the screen so that half of it faces the other way – for face-to-face conversations (as shown in the rightmost image on the previous page).

Set up **Favourite** phrases – one's that you might use frequently and want to avoid saying/typing over and over.

Simply tap the star symbol underneath a translation to add it to Favourites.

Your Favourites are then found by tapping the **Favourites** option at bottom right of the app. You will see the English phrase and the translation for each Favourite.

If you see a sign that needs translating, the Translation app can help.

Tap the camera option at the bottom, and point the lens at the sign, then tap the circle to translate the sign. You can then tap on a paragraph to see the translated text at the bottom of the screen.

16. Speaking the language

If you have an internet connection at the time you want to translate something, you simply ask Siri to do the translation – which will use the Translate app.

There's lots more to explore in the Translate App – but we'll leave you to do this further exploration on your own. Hopefully the above descriptions give you an adequate starting point.

Other Translation apps

Microsoft and Google also have similar apps for translation:

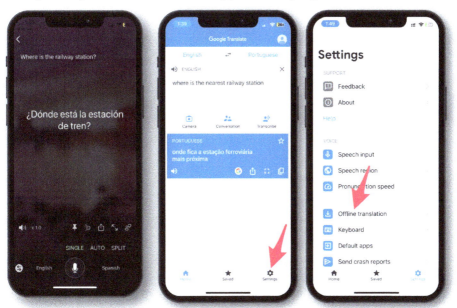

- **Microsoft Translator** (below left)
- **Google Translate** (below middle and right)

Of these two alternative apps, only **Google Translate** provides the option to download Offline translation files (from the app's Settings option – see middle and right images below). Microsoft's app does not *yet* provide this feature.

So, for me, it will be a combination of the Apple and Google translation apps that I will use during our travels.

Here is an article that compares these translation apps: https://appletoolbox.com/apple-translate-vs-google-translate-ios/. Note that the features of such apps are constantly evolving, so this article may not reflect latest features.

16. Speaking the language

Another translation tip

When you travel through Europe – especially in Italy – you will find that you come across lots of Roman Numerals. And I will be honest in saying that I am not all that good at quickly translating a number in Roman Numerals to its decimal equivalent.

For example, what year is represented by the above numerals?

Luckily, there is an app for that!

I have downloaded a free App called **Roman Numerals – Converter**.

Below is the apps' icon.

I can type in the letters that I am seeing to work out the decimal number – or go the other way, typing in a number to see its Roman equivalent.

Very handy!

17. Getting around

Using your mobile for navigation

Whether you are walking around the city, catching public transport, or driving a car, one of the must-haves from a technology perspective is an app for navigation and maps.

The two main apps for navigation using an iPhone are Apple's **Maps** app and the **Google Maps** app.

Apple's Maps is not bad, but a lot of people prefer Google Maps. It is well worth having both apps available on your iPhone.

Both apps require mobile data to refresh the maps as you move. While the built-in GPS does not need internet to track your location, internet is required for the map of your current location to download and refresh.

But what if you don't have mobile data to provide this internet service as you travel?

Pre-load Maps for Offline Navigation

As with translation files, you can choose to download 'offline' maps when you have access to Wi-Fi, so that no mobile internet is needed for navigation and maps.

At the time of writing this book, Apple's **Maps** app doesn't offer this, but **Google Maps** does.

(Note. Reports are that iOS 17 will deliver this feature to Apple Maps in late 2023.)

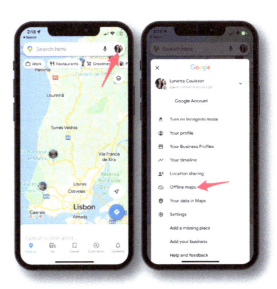

17. Getting around

Tap your account circle at top right, then choose **Offline maps** (see images on previous page).

You will then be able to select the Map area that you wish to download.

Be aware that the bigger the map area you select, the larger the downloaded file – so you will need sufficient available storage for any such file.

In the example below (left-most image), my downloaded Map would require 185MB of space (and will take a while to download).

Once that Map is downloaded, I can see the area it covers by turning off my Wi-Fi and Mobile Data. In the example on the far right below, you can see that the map detail cuts out near Aveiro.

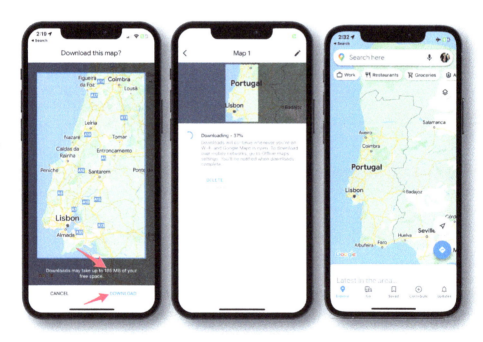

Note that Google Maps won't provide transit information with downloaded maps.

Also, offline maps that you download are removed after 30 days – so you won't need to remember to clean them up.

17.   Getting around

Other Apps for Maps / Navigation

There are other apps to consider for offline navigation, a few of which are **Maps.me**, **HERE WeGo Maps**, and **Sygic**.

I used **Sygic** on our last European trip (for driving/navigation in France and England) and it was excellent. It offers a 3-month Premium+ subscription for $19.99.

Maps.ME is another excellent free app that I will try out on the next trip.

Again, you download maps for your travel locations so that you can use the maps offline when you don't have internet. Tap on the country name to see the Download option.

HERE WeGo Maps is another app that gets a good review and that I will try out.

It wasn't so obvious how to download the offline maps in that last one. You must swipe up the **Where to** area at the bottom of the screen to see more options and see the **Download** option.

Make sure for these apps that you leave the App open while the download of offline maps is completing.

These downloads can take a while. When I downloaded Spain in Maps.me, it took about 45 minutes.

Read about some top GPS app choices at https://www.slashgear.com/1165045/the-5-best-offline-gps-apps-for-iphone-in-2023/

City Guides

Check for any available digital city guides for the places you are visiting – and especially look for offline guides that allow you to explore and learn about the sights without internet.

Here's what came up in App Store for the search phrase City Guide Lisbon.

17. Getting around

Also look for any public transport maps for the city. The **CityMapper** app is popular, but only covers select places – so make sure it is relevant to your trip.

Consider also if you can pre-download any **Audio Guides** of key places/attractions – to save having to purchase such a guide at the location.

Getting from A To B

If you are looking at options for getting from one place to another, there is an excellent website and app that can help.

The app is called **Rome2Rio**, and the website is www.rome2rio.com.

It partners with the likes of Booking.com and Skyscanner for tickets, hotels, and car hire, and with Omio (mentioned below) for train tickets.

Below is an example of the results that I got (on the website) when searching options for getting from Lisbon to Porto in Portugal.

If I click on any of the options presented in the left sidebar, I then get a list of further options – for example, for the train option, I get a list of train times.

For transport that can be booked online in advance, there will be the option to jump to a booking site. Otherwise, the details of how to book with be shown.

17. Getting around

Travel by Car

If you need to grab a ride or rent a car, there are apps and online services that can help with that.

Uber is available in most major cities, for rides to wherever you need to get.

If you haven't used Uber before, make sure to set it up and try it out before you go – and, of course, make sure it is available at your travel destination/s.

Car rentals can be booked online and via an App.

We used a site affiliated with Booking.com – **rentalcars.com**, which also has an app.

Car rental can also be booked through other sites like Webjet, Expedia and other online travel agents.

Train Travel

If you are planning any train trips during your travels, there are some really handy apps for this.

Trainline and **Omio** are excellent apps for booking train tickets in Europe.

Omio also covers the US.

We have used **Trainline** to book tickets in Spain (and checked against Omio). It was easy to do. Note that we needed to provide passport details when booking.

For some train journeys, you will find that there are no options presented if you try to book too far in advance. For our upcoming trip, bookings only open 3 months in advance of the date, so (as mentioned earlier) I have set reminders for those bookings.

17. Getting around

Organising Tours

There are lots of options for exploring and booking available tours at your travel destinations.

Two most commonly used apps/websites for exploring 'what to do' at your destinations and for booking tours are:

- **Viator** (at www.viator.com)

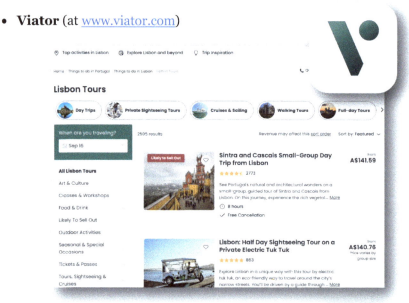

Tripadvisor (www.tripadvisor.com)

17. Getting around

Re-trace your steps

If you have an **Apple Watch**, there is a handy feature worth discovering in the **Compass** app – for helping track your walking route, and then retracing your steps. It is called Waypoints.

By tapping the symbol  in the Compass app (which is bottom left on the screen when viewing your compass – as shown in image on far right), you can set a 'label' for your current location.

Then, at bottom right of the main Compass screen, tap 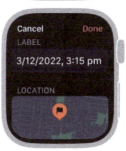 (which is the **Start Backtrack** function) – to start tracing your steps from that place.

Then, tap that spot again to choose to pause your tracing of steps, and to **Retrace Steps**

Tap symbol  at top left to see further information about your current location.

This includes your altitude – something that might be of interest during your travels.

The screen also shows all your 'waypoints' – including where your car is parked, and other locations that you have previously labelled.

18. Accessories

Air tags

I will be adding Apple's **Air Tags** to our checked-in bags (and probably my hand luggage as well).

What is an Air Tag? It is a little accessory (by Apple) that you attach to something valuable. You can then track the location of that Air Tag through the **Find My** app.

Apart from finding lost baggage (or perhaps keys), the attached Air Tag also allows you to monitor your baggage's progress on its way to the collection point – allowing you to perhaps stop for a coffee while waiting for it to get there!

Be Prepared

Don't forget all those adaptors and cables!

Make sure you have all the different types of cables and adaptors that you need for your devices & location.

Consider a multi-port USB adaptor. I have one that offers the different international plugs that can be swapped in and out and provides 4 USB ports.

Another I have just purchased has all the different international plugs built into it and provides both USB-A and USB-C ports.

I also bought a 3-in-1 compact travel charger for Watch, iPhone and AirPods – as well as a case that can hold all the various plugs, adaptors, and cables.

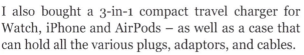

18. Accessories

Stay powered up (and safe) on the go!

Make sure you take at least one portable charger (or power bank) with you (along with a cable) – and make sure you keep it charged up after using it.

As already mentioned in the section starting page 75, portable chargers offer a more secure way of charging your devices.

Plugging your device into public charging stations (via USB) can potentially be risky – especially if, when you plug in, you see a prompt on your device asking you to **Trust** another device - to which you should ALWAYS respond in the negative. If a power point is available, consider using this in preference to a USB port.

As mentioned earlier, my preference is to charge a portable charger at a public USB charging station, then use that charger to charge my device.

I carry a small purse with the charger and associated cables.

Below are a couple of pictures of a new portable charger that I purchased recently, one that has all the necessary charging cables build in to it. Very handy.

It will charge 2-3 iPhones between charges, has a capacity of 10,000 m/Ah, and a rating of 37Wh. And it shows a display of how much charge remains, which is very useful.

18. Accessories

Always consider the Wh rating before carrying a portable/spare battery on a plane, as there are some restrictions that apply – although, in saying this, most portable charges will be well within limits.

While there are International regulations about carrying portable batteries on planes, it is worth double-checking with your airline.

Here is what the Qantas website says about the international regulations on flying with batteries. Note that power banks must be in carry-on baggage.

> ## What you can carry and requirements on how to pack
>
> No more than 20 spare batteries in total, for personal use, are permitted per passenger. All other battery restrictions still apply e.g. no more than two spare lithium batteries exceeding 100Wh and up to 160Wh, are permitted and forms part of the total carried.
>
> A combination of batteries may be carried e.g. 10 x 98Wh lithium ion + 2 x 138Wh lithium ion + 2 x 12V & 98Wh non-spillable + 6 x alkaline.
>
> Note: Watt hours (Wh) are determined by multiplying the voltage (V) by the amp hours (Ah). ie. 12V x 5Ah = 60Wh
>
> **Important**
>
> All spare batteries and powerbanks must be as **carry-on** baggage only.

On Trains Trips

If you are going to be travelling by train, you will find that many trains have power points (and, maybe, USB ports).

So keep a power adaptor and cable in your bag if you are likely to need a charge while on a longer train trip.

AirPods / Headphones

For me, noise cancelling headphones are essential for any travel – especially on flights.

Not all headphones offer noise cancellation.

For example, the standard AirPods from Apple do not offer this feature, but the AirPods Pro do.

I also make sure to take my wired earphones – just in case something happens to my wireless pair.

18. Accessories

Accessory checklist

I'm sure there are a lot of other tech-related accessories that I have left out here. But for what it's worth, here's a bit of a checklist to get you started.

☐ Air Tags

☐ Pin for popping out SIM Card

☐ A small case for carrying your physical SIM (if you need one)

☐ International power plugs

☐ Charging cables and adaptors

☐ Consider multi-port charger

☐ Case for your accessories

☐ Portable battery chargers

☐ Camera adaptor (if you have a separate camera and want to import photos to an iPad or computer)

☐ Headphones – preferably noise cancelling

☐ Take a wired set or earphones for your iPhone - as a spare

☐ Special USB stick for offloading photos – if you have limited storage on your iPhone and might run out of space (see page 130).

19. Your Security While Travelling

Beware on Public Wi-Fi

Always be careful on any public Wi-Fi network that you use while travelling (or even in your home country) - especially airports, cafes, and other public places.

Even your Hotel or accommodation Wi-Fi could be risky.

What is the danger?

There are sometimes hackers, known as sniffers, who sit on public Wi-Fi networks and monitor the traffic, looking for data that is sent across the network in an unencrypted (i.e. unprotected) form.

This data could include, as an example, login credentials for an email (or some other) account, or financial information.

One way to ensure that your uploaded and downloaded data is encrypted as it travels across the Wi-Fi network and internet is to always ensure that the website you are using has a 'lock' on it – that the website's address (URL) starts with **https://**, not **http://**.

http:// sites are not secure, and you should never provide any sign-in credentials, financial, personal or identity information while on such a site.

There is an even better way to make sure that your all internet data is secure while on such a Wi-Fi network.

Use a VPN

The best option for your security is to install something called a VPN – which stands for **Virtual Private Network.**

This VPN should be installed on all devices that will be connected to any public or potentially insecure Wi-Fi networks.

19. Your Security While Travelling

A VPN puts a protective 'layer' (or 'virtual tunnel') around your network connection – encrypting any data you upload or download, thereby creating a secure connection between your device/computer and the network to which it is attached.

This prevents any hackers from being able to read any of the data you sent or receive over that network.

A VPN also disguises your IP Address (which is your internet location), making your location invisible to others – and stopping any tracing of your device.

When you connect to a VPN, it will connect to the closest 'VPN Server' to your current location (a server owned by the VPN provider that you have chosen) – to give the best speed for your internet data uploads and downloads at that location.

Your VPN service provider will have VPN servers in various countries.

You can choose to manually select a 'VPN Server' from a particular country (instead of auto-connecting based on your current location) – including to a server from your home country.

We'll talk about why you might do this shortly.

VPN apps are usually free to install and trial.

After the trial period, a monthly subscription will apply – and this will cover all the devices that use the VPN (perhaps with a limit on how many devices).

As with many Apps and services, you must set up an account with the VPN provider, make sure the provider's App is installed on each device that might connect to an insecure Wi-Fi, and then sign in to the same account on each device (via the App) to use the VPN.

Then, when you need to use Wi-Fi on your travels, you make sure you have turned on this VPN.

Most VPN providers offer a month-by-month subscription OR a multi-month subscription, where the multi-month option is usually at a lower monthly cost.

19. Your Security While Travelling

Some suggestions on VPN

You can use Google to explore the best VPN options for the countries you will be visiting, by typing something like 'best VPN for travel in ....'.

For a long time, **ExpressVPN** has been a top-ranking option, offering services in countries not necessarily covered by other providers (e.g. China).

ExpressVPN will be my choice for our next trip later this year.

Another couple of VPNs that rank very well on all review sites are **NordVPN** and **VPN SurfShark**

I have also previously successfully used a popular option called **Private Internet Access (PIA)**, for a trip through Europe a few years ago.

Monthly subscriptions for VPN services range from $10-$25.

As mentioned earlier, the longer your subscription period, the cheaper the monthly rate.

A special advantage of a VPN

While you travel, you will probably find that your attempts to access your favourite streaming service from back home – e.g. Netflix, ABC iView – are unsuccessful.

This is due to 'geo-blocking' (also known as region blocking), where you are blocked from accessing content from a country that is different to your current location.

A very important benefit of using certain VPNs is that you will be able to 'pretend' you are connected in your home country, and therefore get around this geo-blocking to watch your favourite programs and content from home.

You do this by choosing to connect to a VPN Server located in your home country – and then trying to access your usual streaming content or geo-blocked website.

19. Your Security While Travelling

Not all VPNs are made equal – but ExpressVPN, NordVPN and VPN Surfshark are recommended options if this is something that you are likely to require.

Are your emails secure?

A particular example illustrates the danger of using a device on a public Wi-Fi network without VPN protection.

For some people, the way in which their email is retrieved by their Mail app could be giving away their email address and password to any 'sniffer' on the network.

If you are using an email account such as Bigpond, Optusnet, TPG, iiNet and many others, it is important to check if it your Mail app connects to this account using something called SSL (which encrypts the connection with the mail server so that communications are protected).

For some people, their email account does not have this switch turned on, which means their email address and password will travel over the Wi-Fi without protection. This is only an issue for some accounts that use the connection protocols of POP or IMAP. Accounts like Gmail and Exchange are not impacted.

To check your POP or IMAP account, go to **Settings -> Mail -> Accounts**, and tap on your email account.

If the account shows either IMAP or POP, then it is worth checking the account.

For IMAP accounts, tap the email address showing in the **Account** field.

You will see a screen like that on right with **SMTP** and **Advanced** at the bottom.

19. Your Security While Travelling

Tap the **Advanced** option and check if the **Use SSL** switch is turned on.

For **SMTP**, tap the entry under **PRIMARY SERVER** at the top, and see if SSL is turned on there.

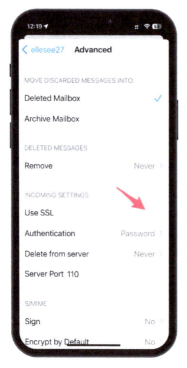
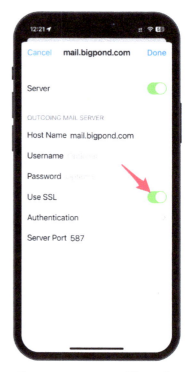

If either SSL switch is turned off, your email account usage will not be secure on a public network.

It is not necessarily a simple matter of turning on that SSL setting and thereby securing your account connection, as the correct **Server Port** needs to be entered as well. And some POP connections will not support SSL.

Incorrect settings in this area will prevent your mail from being received and/or sent.

We won't attempt to provide secure settings for all the different mail providers as part of this book.

If you do need assistance with this, contact your Telco for support – or make an appointment with iTandCoffee.

19. Your Security While Travelling

Always consider your Device Security

When you travel, it is especially important to consider your device security – both physical and virtual.

Make sure that, whenever you enter your device's passcode, you do this in a way that obscures the view for anyone else.

This includes considering any cameras that may be around you, as such cameras could record your passcode entry so that an unscrupulous person could use that recording.

If your device is stolen, it is essential to minimise the risk of the thief knowing or working out your passcode - as that passcode gives them a 'free ride' to wreak all sorts of havoc.

I see many clients who use 4 or 6 digit passcodes for their iPhones, often of poor quality.

Some even choose the option of no passcode, because they find the passcode an annoyance.

These are all very risky practices at the best of times.

Consider this: if the passcode for the device is known to a person who steals your device, there is the option from **Settings** to reset your Apple ID's password!

Yes, the thief only needs your device passcode to change the password for your Apple ID.

Once they have changed this password, you will have lost access to your own Apple ID – and the person will also have access to all the data that is stored in your iCloud, including (perhaps) files from your computer.

They will be able to turn off **Find My** – and prevent you from finding (and wiping) your device using a different device or computer.

The passcode will also provide them with access to the list of passwords that may be stored in **Settings -> Passwords** – meaning that you will be putting other accounts listed there at risk.

They will have access to the email accounts that are installed on that device – and can do all sorts of password resets, contact friends and family, and so much more.

19. Your Security While Travelling

They may even have access to your banking app.

The mind boggles!

Choose a Strong Device Passcode

One of the best protections for your iPhone (and iPad) is a strong passcode.

It is highly recommended that the passcode for your mobile device is as long as possible – and the recommendation is that it is at least 10 numeric or alpha-numeric characters. Mine is 11!

While this may be an inconvenience when unlocking your device, it is well worth that inconvenience for the security it offers.

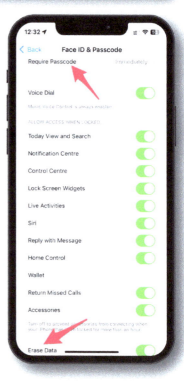

Require Passcode Always and Set Autolock

Make sure that a Passcode (or Face ID / Touch ID) is required as soon as your device goes to sleep.

This means that if someone picks up or steals your phone, it will hopefully already be locked.

To do this, go to **Settings -> Face ID & Passcode** (or **Touch ID & Passcode**).

Make sure **Require Passcode** is set to **Immediately**.

If you have set up Face ID or Touch ID, these can be used instead of the Passcode most of the time. (Note that there must still be a Passcode. You can't have the other forms of authentication without there being an underlying Passcode.)

Also check in **Settings -> Display & Brightness -> Auto-lock**, and make sure the auto-lock period is as low as possible.

19. Your Security While Travelling

This is so that, if the device is not being used, the screen will relatively quickly lock and require the passcode (or Face ID / Touch ID) to then be unlocked.

This also helps conserve your battery, by turning off the display when it is not being used.

Erase After 10 Failed Passcode Attempts

Another protection to consider, especially when you travel, is found in **Settings -> Face ID & Passcode** (or **Touch ID & Passcode**).

Refer to the screen on the previous page, which shows the **Erase Data** option.

With this option turned on, if someone tries 10 times to unlock your device with the wrong passcode, your device will be wiped.

It is quite a drastic option to choose, but certainly offers a very effective protection in the case of theft.

Of course you would only choose such an option if your devices content was being backed and synced with iCloud.

Protecting photos and data

For most of us, our photos are such an important part of our trips – and it is important to consider how to keep these photos safe and secure.

If your photos are only stored on your mobile device and something happens to that device, they could be lost forever.

What can you do to protect them?

19. Your Security While Travelling

One strategy is to sync all your photos to iCloud. Whenever you connect to Wi-Fi, your photos will upload to your iCloud – and be available on any other device that is also connected to that iCloud.

You can also then access your photos from the website **iCloud.com**, by signing in with your Apple ID (which is an email address) and associated password.

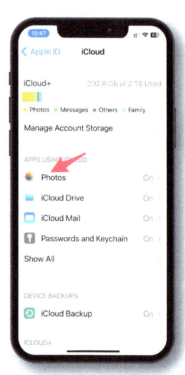

On your iPad and iPhone, check your settings for iCloud photos in **Settings -> *your-name* -> iCloud -> Photos**.

To check that your photos have been uploaded to iCloud, go to the **Photos** app, to the Recents Album.

At the very bottom, you will see a count of your photos and videos, as well as the sync progress.

In the example below right, you can see that my photo syncing with iCloud is up to date.

Another way of protecting your photos and other data stored on your device is to ensure that your device content is backing up to iCloud.

This backup, if enabled, will occur every 24 hours or so, as long as your device is connected to Wi-Fi, locked and charging.

Check your backup settings in **Settings -> *your-name* -> iCloud -> iCloud Backup**.

Syncing your photos and backing up your device to iCloud does require that you have sufficient iCloud storage for that data.

You only get 5GB for free, and that will fill up quickly.

To use iCloud Photos and iCloud Backup, you will most likely need to pay a monthly fee. If you don't have enough storage (which you can check in

19. Your Security While Travelling

Settings -> *your-name* -> iCloud), choose the **Manage Account Storage** option, and then **Change Storage Plan**.

We won't go further into the topics of Photos and iCloud (or iCloud Storage), as these are the topics of other iTandCoffee books and videos.

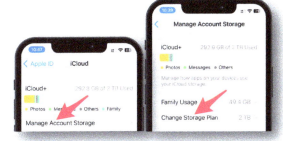

Find My

If you are unlucky enough to lose your iPhone (or iPad) while travelling, there is feature which – if enabled – can allow you to potentially track your device, play a sound to try to find it, lock it with a message on the screen (e.g. providing a number that the finder can call), and erase it remotely.

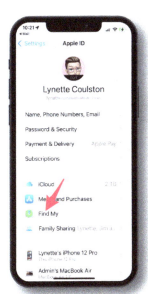
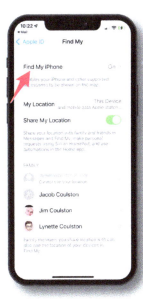

It is the **Find My ...** feature and app. On the iPhone and iPad, you set up this feature in **Settings -> *your-name*** (see leftmost image above). By turning on this feature you may be able to locate the device even if it was muted before you misplaced it, playing a sound that hopefully allows you to find it.

In the worst-case scenario of the device being stolen, **Find My** allows you to perform a remote wipe of your device.

19. Your Security While Travelling

Additionally, by turning on **Find my ...**, you will be locking your device so that, even if someone steals it and they wipe it, that person will not be able to activate the and use wiped device without knowing your iCloud password – thereby rendering the device useless to them.

This is a great theft deterrent introduced by Apple in recent years and has, reportedly, reduced the number of thefts, especially of iPhones.

To ensure that you can find the last place your device was located before the battery died, make sure you also turn on the **Send Last Location** option (see rightmost image on previous page). It is also worth turning on **Find My network** to maximise your chance of finding the device, even if it is offline and/or powered down.

Finding a lost device

To locate a lost device, you can sign into the **Find My** app on another Apple Device; or visit **iCloud.com** on any computer, sign in with your Apple ID and password, and choose the **Find iPhone** option.

As mentioned above, a relatively new option now available in the **Find My** settings is the **Find My network**. Here's how Apple describes this option.

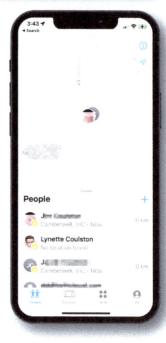

> *"The Find My network is a crowdsourced network of hundreds of millions of Apple devices that can help users locate a missing iPhone, iPad, Mac, Apple Watch and soon, third-party Find My network-enabled accessories, using the Find My app."*

Apple assures us all that your privacy is protected even if you enrol your device in this program.

If you are in an iCloud Family, and if you have shared your location with your family members (something that is an option), another member of your family can use the **Find My** app on their own device to locate your device.

On the iPhone (and iPad), **the Find My** app provides four options along the bottom – **People**, **Devices**, **Items**, and **Me**.

19. Your Security While Travelling

It is from the **Devices** option that you can locate a lost device – either your own or, depending on setup, those belonging to members of your iCloud Family (again, only if they have chosen to share their device's location with you).

The devices are shown on a map that can be zoomed in and out (see below) and listed below that map.

 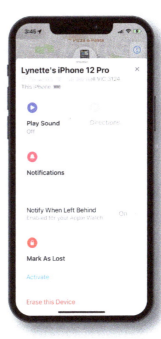

Tap any device to select it and see options for locating that device.

- **Play Sound** to send a loud noise (like a radar signal) to the device, which will play even if the device is muted or has low volume.

- **Mark as Lost** if you don't know where it is and want to provide your contact details and a message to someone who finds it (choose Activate to use this option).

- **Erase this Device** if the device is not retrievable.

20. Must-have apps

So many apps!

Of course, there are so many apps to choose from when it comes to travel.

We have already mentioned many in earlier chapters and will mention a few more shortly.

Here is a summarized list of some of the more popular apps.

- ☐ Tripit – travel planner / itinerary.
- ☐ Trainline, Omio – train tickets.
- ☐ Rome2Rio – options for getting from A to B (plus bookings).
- ☐ Booking.com – accommodation, flights, car rentals.
- ☐ AirBNB – accommodation.
- ☐ Expedia.com - accommodation, flights, car rentals.
- ☐ Skyscanner – aggregator of flight, hotel, car rental options.
- ☐ Tripadviser – all things travel – hotels, restaurants, tours.
- ☐ Trivago – aggregator of hotel options.
- ☐ Viator – what to see and do.
- ☐ Citymapper – Public transport app and maps.
- ☐ Visit a City – what to do.
- ☐ Apple Translate – offline or online translations.
- ☐ Google Translate - offline or online translations.
- ☐ Microsoft Translator – online translations only.
- ☐ Airline app/s.
- ☐ Google Maps – maps and navigation.
- ☐ Airalo – data only eSIMs.
- ☐ Mobile banking app/s.
- ☐ Insurance Company app (if applicable).
- ☐ Sygic – maps and navigation.
- ☐ Maps.ME – maps and navigation.
- ☐ Uber – car rides.
- ☐ XE Currency – currency conversion.

20. Must-have apps

☐   Camera+ - fantastic photo optimization.

☐   Scannable or Adobe Scan – scanning using your mobile.

☐   Adobe Fill & Sign – fill forms and sign forms/documents.

☐   A good Weather app (e.g. Yahoo Weather).

☐   Flush - public toilet finder!!

Scanning documents

Make sure you have a scanning app on your iPhone, for any situation where you need to scan a physical page (or pages) to send to someone.

My go-to app scanning app has been, for many years, Scannable by Evernote, which is a free app.

Another excellent free option is Adobe Scan.

These apps are not just relevant to travel. They are must-haves for any mobile device and can save you from ever having to fire up that printer/scanner ever again.

Signing documents while away

An app mentioned in the above list is a 'must-have' for travelling – in fact, for any time.

I use it whenever I need to fill in and sign a form.

It is the **Adobe Fill and Sign** app, which allows you to so easily fill and sign forms and documents without needing to involve a printer or scanner.

You can even save you signature for re-use whenever it is needed.

If you have an iPad, it is worth taking a stylus – or even better, an Apple Pencil – for signing anything while you are away.

20. Must-have apps

Discover the Health App

Your iPhone can track your steps as you walk around (as can your Apple Watch, of course).

Your daily steps can then be viewed in the **Health** app, one of Apple standard apps.

It is amazing to see, at the end of a day of walking, just how many steps you have taken!

As mentioned in chapter 9. make sure you set up your **Medical ID** in the **Health** app.

21. What about money

There are a few key things to think about in relation to money and technology when you are travelling – as well as some key things that are not really technology related, but that are worthy of a mention.

Do you get SMS Authorisations?

As mentioned earlier, if you get SMS authorisations from your bank, make sure you have access to your home SIM for texted codes. As also covered earlier, you will also need to have access to International Roaming to receive any such SMS.

Let the bank know your plans

Make sure you notify your bank that you will be away.

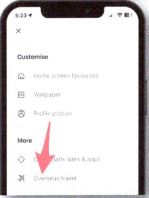

Otherwise, your use of your credit/debit card while overseas could result in your account being frozen due to suspected fraud.

For some banks such a notification can be done from within the bank's mobile App.

Such options may be found under the **Cards** option of the banking app, or (as for Commbank) in the **Setting**s area.

Screens from the Commbank app are shown on the right.

Travel money

If you use your usual credit or debit card while travelling, you will find that every transaction incurs an international transaction fee – and the cost of these fees can mount up over time.

Another option to consider is a special travel debit card, one that you load up with the currency (or currencies) you will need while you travel. This card can then be topped up as needed.

21. What about money

Several banks offer such travel money cards. Westpac's gets the best review for fees/etc. Here's a **choice.com** article on the topic: www.choice.com.au/travel/money/travel-money/articles/travel-money-cards

I use the **Commbank Travel Card** because I am a Commbank customer – and I can manage this card from within my usual Commbank app.

It is so quick & easy to transfer money immediately, between my normal account and the travel card – and choose a currency when I do this. The exchange rate that applies at the time shows.

I add money to this travel card account on a regular basis before the trip, on days when the exchange rate is good.

I also have a **Qantas Travel Money** card – a debit card that is linked to my Qantas Frequent Flyer account. This will also have a bit of money on it as backup.

For the Qantas card, there is an app that allows easy top-up of funds of any currency. The downside of the Qantas card is that there is a 1 day delay for free top-ups (using the bank transfer option) – and its exchange rate is always lower than the Commbank app.

Wise is another highly rated travel money card to consider.

Just make sure before you go that you have any relevant app associated with your Travel Money Card, and that you know how to top up.

Just as a note, Commbank provided me with two Travel cards for the one account, so that I have a spare – just in case!

Tracking the exchange rate

If you are looking to load up a travel money card in advance of your trip on days when the exchange rate is good, it is worth setting up currency exchange rate alerts.

I get an alert each morning that advises of the day's exchange rate. That alert pops up as a notification and can also arrive in an email.

The app I have used to get my daily alert is the **Wise** app – the app associated with the Wise travel money card. You don't have use one of their cards to take advantage of this feature.

21. What about money

Here are other apps that provide alerts. A couple of examples are:

- **CurrencyXT**– no need to create an account to get rate alerts.
- **XE Currency** – you must create account to get rate alerts.

All of the above-mentioned apps allow you to view how the exchange rate tracks over time.

Note. **XE Currency** has been my 'go to' app for currency conversion for over 12 years.

You may still need a credit card for certain things

It is important to note that, while your travel money debit card will be accepted in most places, there are a few circumstances where you might need a credit card instead.

For example, when checking in for a hotel room, or when hiring a car, you may have to provide a credit card for incidentals.

So, make sure you take your usual credit card as well – or perhaps take an alternative credit card to your usual card, one that has a limited credit limit.

Travel Cards and Apple Pay

I found that for Qantas and Commbank travel cards, you can't add the cards to your Wallet for Apple Pay, so you can't just use your iPhone to pay using these cards.

You will instead need to carry these physical cards.

Travel Insurance

Does your credit card provide travel insurance with it?

Some credit cards offer such insurance, so make sure you investigate this option. It could save you lots.

22. Your Travel Snaps

Capturing those holiday memories

What will you use to take photos while you travel? Most of us tend you just take our mobile phones as our camera.

We have already talked about a couple of things relating to your photos – storage and backups or syncing.

But let's look at some other things to consider.

Taking a separate camera?

Will you take a separate digital camera?

Will you want to import to an iPad or computer while you travel?

If yes, you may need an adaptor for that. Don't forget to pack it.

Make sure Camera saves locations

One of the best reasons for using your smartphone to take photos is that such photos can record the exact location of the photo.

This is so useful when you travel, because it allows for viewing of your travel snaps on a map and later allows you to work out where they were taken.

Go to **Settings -> Privacy & Security -> Location Services -> Camera**.

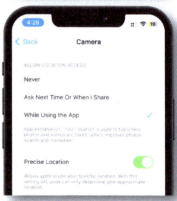

Make sure that in the section headed **ALLOW LOCATION ACCESS**, there is a tick against the **While Using the App** option.

Also turn on **Precise Location** while you travel, so that your photos do show exactly where they were taken.

22. Your Travel Snaps

Sharing Photos

Do you want to share your photos with others while you travel (or after)? How do you plan to do this?

Shared iCloud Albums

There is a great iCloud feature called **Shared Albums.**

This feature allows you to create an album of photos in your iCloud, one that other people can also see via their own **Photos** app or via their web browser.

This shared album can be added to after creation – both by the person who created it, and (optionally) by those with whom it has been shared.

Any Apple user who you have invited to share your Shared Album can post comments about the photos via the Photos app – and these comments are then seen by others who also share that Shared Album.

These Shared Albums do not contribute to your iCloud storage allowance.

We won't attempt to cover further details about Shared Albums as part of this book, as it is covered in detail in other iTandCoffee books and videos about the Photos app. Contact iTandCoffee to learn more.

Airdrop

If you are travelling with others who use Apple devices, another handy option for sharing photos is AirDrop – where you send content from your device to another nearby person's device.

No internet connection is required for Airdrop.

Each device must be connected to Wi-Fi and have Bluetooth turned on. And they must be in close proximity.

22. Your Travel Snaps

The receiving device must be open for receiving of Airdropped content, an option that can be adjusted from **Control Centre** or from **Settings -> General -> Airdrop**.

Set this to **Everyone for 10 Minutes** to ensure that the other sending device can 'see' the receiving the device.

Then, the sender simply selects the photos that need to be shared, chooses the Share ⬆ symbol and then **Airdrop**. The devices that can receive content will be listed.

Tap the other person's device to immediately send the photo/s (or video/s) to them.

Share an iCloud Link

And there is also the option to select a set of photos, choose the **Share** ⬆ option, then choose **Copy iCloud Link**. This copies a link to your device's clipboard.

Paste the created link into an iMessage (or email) to another person. That person can then tap/click the link to view the photos on an Apple web page, and choose to view or download the photos to their own Photos app.

Taking great photos

Make sure you know how to take good photos with your iPhone.

Always ensure the lens in clean, and that you focus it correctly before taking any shot.

If needed, tap on the screen, on the object you want to use as the focus, then take the shot.

When you take selfies, use the **Timer** feature of Camera – to avoid having to reach with your free hand to press that dot. You can choose the 3 second or 10 second timer, to so that you have time to position yourself and get the right smile on your face!

Discover the panoramic photos feature of the Camera app, for all those scenery and wide angle shots.

22. Your Travel Snaps

And sometimes it is worth considering a third-party app for some quick touch-ups and edits.

For many years, I have used an app called **Camera+**, because it does amazing enhancements of images with a single tap, to really make your photos 'pop'.

Below is such an example, with the right-hand image showing the image after Camera+ 'clarified' it.

Use Camera for signs, timetables

Remember to use your iPhone or iPad camera to capture timetables and signs, so that you can refer back to them.

Use the Camera to translate signs

If you see a sign in another language, point your camera at it. You will see some yellow brackets appear around the area of identified by the Camera as text.

22. Your Travel Snaps

Tap the symbol at bottom right (see the example image on the previous page).

Then tap 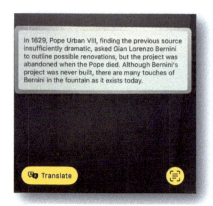 to see the translation – as shown on the right.

The applicable language will be automatically determined.

Note that you will need internet for this to work – either Wi-Fi or mobile data.

Limited Storage for Photos?

Your iPhone may not have enough space for all your photos – no matter how hard you try to free up space.

One option to consider is to use a device for backing up your Photos, and then removing them from the iPhone (or iPad) to free up space.

SanDisk has the iXpand device – which plugs into both iPhone/iPad and a computer. It has the lightning connector AND the USB-A connector.

Here is an article about exporting to a Flash Drive (USB), if you are interested in learning more: https://www.technewstoday.com/how-to-transfer-photos-from-iphone-to-flash-drive/

Organising photos as you go

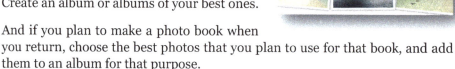

If you have time at the end of each day, or when in transit, it is well worth going through recent photos and cleaning up any that you don't need, or applying edits where needed.

Create an album or albums of your best ones.

And if you plan to make a photo book when you return, choose the best photos that you plan to use for that book, and add them to an album for that purpose.

If you use a service like Snapfish for making photo books, you can even progressively upload your chosen photos (when you have Wi-Fi) – so that you don't need to go through this process when you return.

23. Entertainment

Movies and TV Series on your device

If you have sufficient storage on an iPad (or perhaps even on an iPhone) it may be worth downloading some movies, TV series or documentaries – so that you can watch them without requiring internet.

Some streaming services allow you to download content. Or there is always the option to purchase content from the iTunes store.

For your listening pleasure

If you have Apple Music, make sure your favourite music is downloaded, so that you don't need internet to stream it.

Again, you will need sufficient storage for this.

If you are a Spotify user, the same applies – and you will need a paid plan to do this with Spotify.

Another great option for travelling is **Podcasts** – which are usually completely free. Again, make sure you download a set of podcasts before you go, or when you have access to Wi-Fi.

Reading

If you are an avid reader, carrying a range of books with you as you travel can really add to the weight and bulk of your luggage.

An alternative option that allows you to take as many books as you like – without impacting your luggage – is to read **eBooks**.

23. Entertainment

eBooks can be read on your iPad or iPhone, using the Apple-provided Books app.

If you prefer Amazon's eBook service, you can use the Kindle app on your Apple devices.

But one of the things that has frustrated me about reading on my iPhone or iPad is that

a) the battery depletes too quickly,

b) if I am outside, the device gets very hot quickly, and

c) the display will dim in the bright light and make it hard to read.

So I recently purchased a **Kindle** device. It is very light, has a battery that lasts for about 10 weeks, can be read in the sun and on the beach, and is even waterproof.

I will download a set of books in advance and as we travel (when on Wi-Fi).

There are a couple other key benefits of eBooks. You can download samples of books to read the first set of pages, to see if you like it before purchasing. And many of the classics are free to download and read.

Other Entertainment

Finally, think about downloading some time-wasters from the App Store – games and puzzles that help to fill in time in transit, and while waiting.

Some good examples are:

- Solitaire
- Sudoku
- Wordle
- Quordle
- Jigsaws
- Crosswords
- Threes
- Tetris
- Angry Birds

(Note that some of these require internet.)

Appendix A
International Roaming with Telstra

Telstra offers two main services for International Roaming, for most people with monthly post-paid Telstra plans – **International Day Pass** and **Pay As You Go.**

International Day Pass

https://www.telstra.com.au/content/dam/tcom/help/critical-information-summaries/personal/mobile/international-roaming/International-Day-Pass.pdf

- Pay per day - $5 (New Zealand) or $10 for long list of other countries (check the countries that it covers before you leave).
- You are only charged on days where you use your phone, send a text, or use mobile data.
- On days you use the day pass, you have unlimited calls/texts & 1GB data
- Data is automatically topped up if you use > 1gb in a day, and top-up is then valid for 31 days. The 1GB daily allowance does not roll over – it expires each day.
- Activate (or de-activate) Day Pass using My Telstra App. Note that there is a delay in de-activating and activating – it is not immediate.
- You will receive data usage warnings via text, at 50%, 85%, 100%.
- The 'day' is based on AEST, not local OS time - AEST 0:00 TO 24:00.

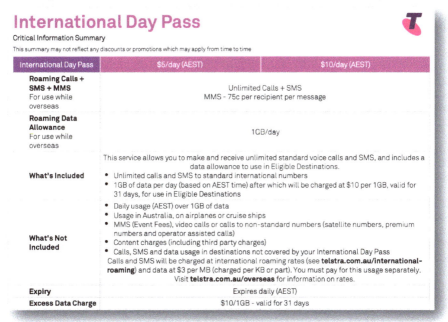

International Day Pass
Critical Information Summary
This summary may not reflect any discounts or promotions which may apply from time to time

International Day Pass	$5/day (AEST)	$10/day (AEST)
Roaming Calls + SMS + MMS For use while overseas	Unlimited Calls + SMS MMS - 75c per recipient per message	
Roaming Data Allowance For use while overseas	1GB/day	
What's Included	This service allows you to make and receive unlimited standard voice calls and SMS, and includes a data allowance to use in Eligible Destinations. • Unlimited calls and SMS to standard international numbers • 1GB of data per day (based on AEST time) after which will be charged at $10 per 1GB, valid for 31 days, for use in Eligible Destinations	
What's Not Included	• Daily usage (AEST) over 1GB of data • Usage in Australia, on airplanes or cruise ships • MMS (Event Fees), video calls or calls to non-standard numbers (satellite numbers, premium numbers and operator assisted calls) • Content charges (including third party charges) • Calls, SMS and data usage in destinations not covered by your International Day Pass Calls and SMS will be charged at international roaming rates (see **telstra.com.au/international-roaming**) and data at $3 per MB (charged per KB or part). You must pay for this usage separately. Visit **telstra.com.au/overseas** for information on rates.	
Expiry	Expires daily (AEST)	
Excess Data Charge	$10/1GB - valid for 31 days	

Appendix A
International Roaming with Telstra

Countries covered by the $10 Day Pass are (as at the time of writing this book):

Argentina, Austria, Bangladesh, Belarus, Belgium, Brazil, Brunei, Bulgaria, Cambodia, Canada, Chile, China, Colombia, Croatia, Cyprus, Czech Republic, Denmark, Ecuador, Egypt, Estonia, Fiji, Finland, France, Germany, Greece, Hong Kong, Hungary, India, Indonesia, Ireland, Israel, Italy, Japan, Laos, Latvia, Lithuania, Luxembourg, Macau, Macedonia, Malaysia, Mexico, Nauru, Netherlands, Norway, Papua New Guinea, Philippines, Poland, Portugal, Qatar, Romania, Russia, Saudi Arabia, Serbia, Singapore, Slovak Rep., Slovenia, Solomon Islands, South Africa, South Korea, Spain, Sri Lanka, Sweden, Switzerland, Taiwan, Thailand, Turkey, Ukraine, UAE, UK, USA, Uruguay, Vanuatu, Vietnam

IMPORTANT NOTE: Cruise ships are excluded from Day Pass - PAYG rates apply.

Pay As You Go (PAYG)

International Roaming defaults to PAYG if the Day Pass option is disabled, and in locations with the Day Pass is not available.

Be very careful of ever using PAYG. You need to make sure you know how to avoid unexpected calls and data costs.

Never use PAYG if mobile data and data roaming are active.

- You pay per mb of data ($3/MB) and for each call ($2-$3.50 per min) & sent SMS (75¢ per standard text, >$3/mb for MMS).
- This can result in huge expense, so beware.
- Rates for calls vary depending on location.
- I suggest only using PAYG if you want to do occasional SMS's (or if you have no other option).
- Rates vary based on overseas location – here is where to check your destination's costs: *https://www.telstra.com.au/international-roaming/lightbox-international-roaming-rates-map*

Appendix A
International Roaming with Telstra

Here are some examples of the costs for the different countries, as applied at the time of writing this book.

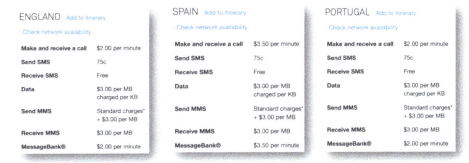

As you can see, data roaming (which includes messages that use MMS) is very expensive. And the cost of any incoming or outgoing phone call can end up being well above the Day Pass cost (if that is an option for you).

Managing International Roaming with Telstra

- Get the **My Telstra** app from the App Store.
- Activate/manage roaming via this **My Telstra** app.
- Select **Services** at bottom, then tap your mobile service, then tap **Extras** (at top).

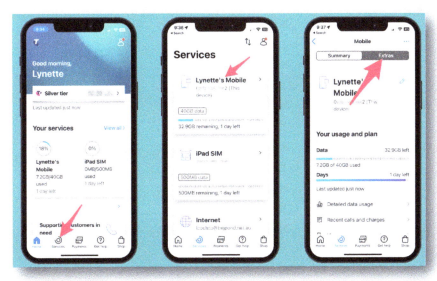

Appendix A
International Roaming with Telstra

- Choose the **International Roaming** option to see what settings are available.

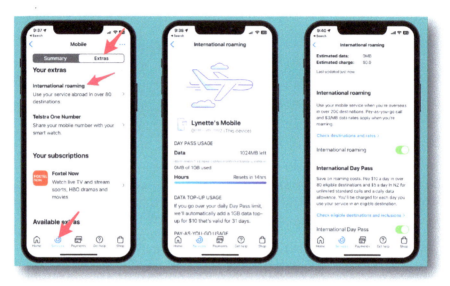

- You will hopefully see the **International roaming** switch and a separate **International Day Pass** switch underneath that.
- If **International Day Pass** is turned off and **International** Roaming is on, **PAYG** applies if there are any calls, outgoing texts or mobile data used.

Pre-paid Roaming Packs (for pre-paid SIM)

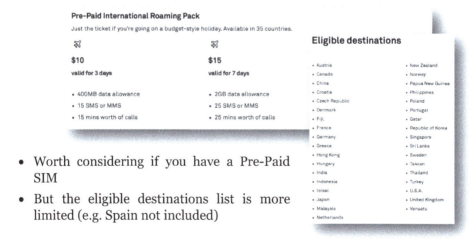

- Worth considering if you have a Pre-Paid SIM
- But the eligible destinations list is more limited (e.g. Spain not included)

Appendix B
International Roaming with Optus

Optus $5 Roaming Add-On

https://www.optus.com.au/mobile/plans/international-roaming

- Optus has similar offerings to Telstra.
- But Optus is half the price and has a more generous data allowance (5GB per day).
- The **Roaming Add-on** is enabled via the **My Optus** app.
- It offers unlimited standard talk & text and 5GB of data per day, for 100+ countries.

The key difference in the Optus offering is that

- $5 Roaming Add-on must be enabled on each day that you want to use it – from the app.
- Or you can choose a 7-day option for $35, so that you don't have to enable each day.
- Wi-Fi connection is not needed to enable the add-on for the day – so you can do this on the go.
- Availability of the Add-on depends on your plan. Available to Optus Choice Plus, Optus Plus Family & Optus Plus

Set up your $5 Roaming Add-on

Open My Optus App to check your roaming options under:

Service > Add-ons > International Roaming

Your roaming add-on starts on activation it so it's best to buy it on arrival, at your destination.
(No Wi-Fi required).

Choose and buy a roaming add-on. Grab your bags – you're good to go.

As you return home to Australia, roaming will automatically switch off. Thanks for roaming with us.

Appendix B
International Roaming with Optus

- Check if your destination is covered:

A	G	M	S
Albania	Georgia	Macao	Samoa (Western)
Argentina	Germany	Macedonia	San Marino
Armenia	Greece	Malaysia	Serbia
Austria	Greenland	Malta	Singapore
Azerbaijan	Guam	Mexico	Slovakia
B	Guernsey	Moldova	Slovenia
Bangladesh	**H**	Montenegro	Solomon Islands
Belarus	Hong Kong	Myanmar*	South Africa
Belgium	Hungary	**N**	Spain
Bosnia and Herzegovina	**I**	Nauru	Sri Lanka
Brazil	Iceland	Netherlands	Sweden
Bulgaria	India	New Zealand	Switzerland
C	Indonesia	Norway	**T**
Cambodia	Ireland	**P**	Taiwan, Province of China
Canada	Isle of Man	Pakistan	Tajikistan
Chile	Israel	Palestine	Thailand
China	Italy	Panama	Timor
Colombia	**J**	Papua New Guinea	Tonga
Croatia	Japan	Philippines	Turkey
Cyprus	Jersey	Poland	**U**
Czech Republic	**K**	Portugal	Ukraine
D	Kazakhstan	Puerto Rico	United Arab Emirates
Denmark	Korea, Republic of	**Q**	United Kingdom
E	Kuwait	Qatar	United States
Ecuador	Kyrgyzstan	**R**	US Virgin Islands
Estonia	**L**	Romania	**V**
F	Latvia	Russian Federation	Vanuatu
Faroe Islands	Liechtenstein		Vatican City (Holy See)
Fiji	Lithuania		Vietnam
Finland	Luxembourg		
France			
French Polynesia			

- Different costs apply for some plans (non Choice Plus) plans.
- Make sure you know what plan you are on and consider an upgrade if you don't qualify.

- For other plans, cost is $10 per day for the **Roaming Pass** (instead of $5)
- Check your roaming options from the **Service** option of the My Optus app (along bottom of app),
  Service > Settings > International Roaming

Appendix B
International Roaming with Optus

- Note that PAYG rates apply if the Roaming Add-on is not available.

Pay as You Go

- If you are not using the daily add-on/pass, PAYG Rates apply and are $1-$2 per MB for data, $1.5-$4 /min for talk, 50¢-$1 per sent SMS.

Postpaid roaming rates

Location	Data	Talk	Text
Zone 1	$1/MB	$1.50/min	50c/SMS
Zone 2	$1/MB	$1.50/min	50c/SMS
Zone 3	$2/MB	$4.00/min	$1/SMS

- Determine the Zone/costs applicable to your travel destination at *https://www.optus.com.au/mobile/plans/international-roaming/postpaid-rates*

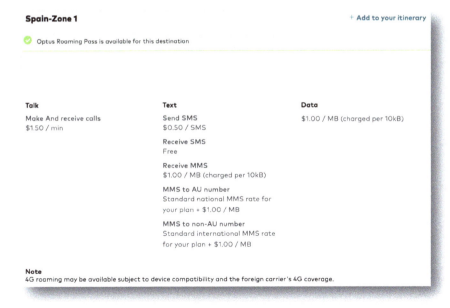

Spain-Zone 1

\+ Add to your itinerary

✅ Optus Roaming Pass is available for this destination

Talk
Make And receive calls
$1.50 / min

Text
Send SMS
$0.50 / SMS

Receive SMS
Free

Receive MMS
$1.00 / MB (charged per 10kB)

MMS to AU number
Standard national MMS rate for your plan + $1.00 / MB

MMS to non-AU number
Standard international MMS rate for your plan + $1.00 / MB

Data
$1.00 / MB (charged per 10kB)

Note
4G roaming may be available subject to device compatibility and the foreign carrier's 4G coverage.

Appendix B
International Roaming with Optus

Prepaid Roaming Options

https://www.optus.com.au/mobile/plans/international-roaming/prepaid

- If you have pre-paid SIM, you also have $5 and $35 roaming options, but there are different inclusions to those for post-paid accounts.

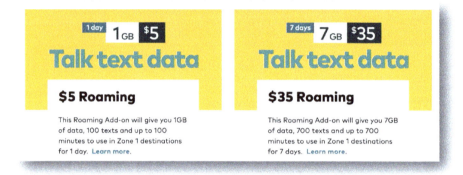

- $5 roaming has 1GB of data, 100 texts and up to 100 mins talk per day.
- $35 roaming has 7GB of data, 700 texts and up to 700 minutes per 7 days.
- Only available for Zone 1 countries
- Credits are also available - $10 talk credit, $20 data-only credit for limited destinations. See link above for further details.

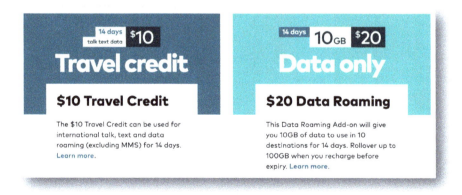

Handy article about Optus Roaming

- *www.whistleout.com.au/MobilePhones/Guides/Optus-international-roaming-everything-you-need-to-know*

Appendix C
International Roaming with Vodafone

$5 Roaming

https://www.vodafone.com.au/plans/international-roaming

- Like Optus, Vodafone offers a $5/day option.
- The key difference with Vodafone is that it that uses your usual plan's call and data inclusions.
- Use the **My Vodafone app** to check and manage this.

How $5 Roaming works

$5 extra a day

You'll only be charged $5 extra a day in addition to your plan fees when you use your included data, make or receive a call or send an SMS.

Use your plan overseas

Use your plan's included data, calls and texts in over 100 countries. Excludes data capped at speeds of up to 1.5Mbps, 2Mbps, 10Mbps and 25Mbps. If you go over your included data limit, we'll automatically add 1GB for $5.

Easy activation

$5 Roaming should be activated already for you. Just switch on your phone in an eligible country. You can check and manage roaming through My Vodafone.

- Check if $5 Roaming is offered for your destination.

Appendix C
International Roaming with Vodafone

Pay As You Go

https://www.vodafone.com.au/support/plans/roaming-rates

- PAYG option is also available - $1/min, 75¢ for outbound SMS, $1 per MB data.
- See above map for countries that only offer this option.
- As for other Telco's, be very cautious of turning on Mobile Data and Roaming if you choose the PAYG option.

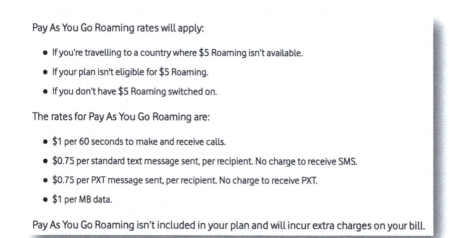

Pay As You Go Roaming rates will apply:

- If you're travelling to a country where $5 Roaming isn't available.
- If your plan isn't eligible for $5 Roaming.
- If you don't have $5 Roaming switched on.

The rates for Pay As You Go Roaming are:

- $1 per 60 seconds to make and receive calls.
- $0.75 per standard text message sent, per recipient. No charge to receive SMS.
- $0.75 per PXT message sent, per recipient. No charge to receive PXT.
- $1 per MB data.

Pay As You Go Roaming isn't included in your plan and will incur extra charges on your bill.

Prepaid Roaming

https://www.vodafone.com.au/prepaid/plans/international-roaming

- If you have (or get) a Pre-paid SIM from Vodafone, you can choose a Prepaid Roaming Add-on

- Pre-pay for calls and data – e.g. $5 for 1 day, with 25 mins talk, 30 outbound texts and 200MB data; $35 for 7 days, 200 mins talk, 300 texts, 2GB data.

Appendix C
International Roaming with Vodafone

- Recharge using a text code.
- Make sure to check if your destination is covered.

There are over 80 countries where you can use a Prepaid Roaming Add-on. See the full list of countries below. These countries may change from time to time, so it's important to check that your chosen country is included.

Prepaid Roaming Add-on countries

Cruising

- Vodafone may have Maritime Roaming rates for your cruise ship.
- $5 per mins talk, 75¢ per outbound texts, $1 per MB data.

Maritime Roaming

Maritime Roaming rates may apply if you're on a cruise, even if it's only around Australia. On selected cruise ships, you can make calls, send text messages and use data at the following rates:

- $5 per 60 seconds to make and receive calls.
- $0.75 per standard text message sent, per recipient. No charge to receive SMS.
- $1.00 per MB.

We have roaming partnerships with Telenor Maritime and Wireless Maritime Services. Check their websites to see if Maritime Roaming is available on your cruise ship. If it's available, on-board Wi-Fi is an alternative to using mobile data.

Appendix D
Managing Multiple SIMs

While managing multiple SIMS is not a topic just related to travel, it may well be your travel that is the reason why you first explore the use of multiple SIMs.

So let's look at how you might manage these SIMs to avoid excess charges when you travel.

In the scenarios I will describe below, I have a SIM named **Telstra** that is my usual, home SIM (a Telstra SIM on a post-paid plan) and another SIM that I have purchased for my trip, which I have named **Travel**.

Let's take a look at the steps involved in managing which SIM (or SIMs) are used for voice/SMS and mobile data, in **Settings -> Mobile**.

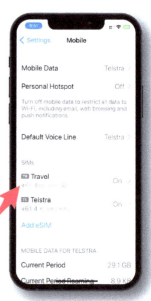

Scenario 1: Two SIMs active – no need to restrict mobile data or phone/SMS use

First let's look at the scenario where you have two SIMs active – as shown in the image on right and where I am not trying to restrict my use of either.

The section headed **SIMs**, shows that both the Travel and Telstra SIM are **On**.

With two SIMs active at the same time, I must make the following choices:

- which SIM is to be used for **Mobile Data** (first option in top image on right) and
- which is the **Default Voice Line**.

Enabling two SIMs

To enable the SIMs that I want to use, I must tap each applicable SIM under the SIMs heading and turn on the **Turn on this Line** switch.

The name of each SIM is configurable. Tap **Mobile Plan Label** (top option in image on right) and choose a standard label from the list, or tap **Custom** to create your own customised label.

Appendix D
Managing Multiple SIMs

Choose which SIM for Mobile Data

In the example on the right, you can see the Telstra SIM is the SIM currently being used for mobile data – which then means that the section further down shows **MOBILE DATA FOR TELSTRA**.

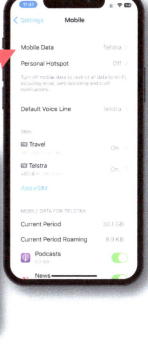

The data usage figures that show in that section will be for that Telstra SIM (not the Travel SIM).

If I want to instead use the Travel SIM for mobile data, I must ensure that the **Mobile Data** field is showing **Travel** – which I change by tapping the Mobile Data field and tapping to choose the Travel SIM instead.

If I want my device to automatically switch to the alternative SIM for mobile data whenever the Default SIM does not have mobile data service, I can enable the **Allow Mobile Data Switching** option (see image above).

I can happily enable this option when I am in my home country but will turn this off this when travelling – so that I can fully control which SIM is allowing using of mobile data.

Choose your Data Mode

When viewing the settings for your SIM (tap the SIM in the **SIMs** section of **Settings->Mobile**), you will see a **Data Mode** setting.

This setting is important when you travel, as it can help you control the amount of mobile data that your device uses.

Appendix D
Managing Multiple SIMs

Consider changing this setting when you travel, to limit the amount of data used for certain activities.

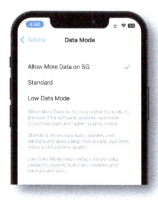

If your iPhone supports 5G connection, your phone may be set to **Allow More Data on 5G.**

Consider setting this mode to **Standard** mode – to limit Video and Facetime quality.

Or to really limit data usage, choose **Low Data Mode** to stop any automatic updates and background tasks (just in case you haven't specifically turned these off).

Choose which SIM for Calls/Messages

When there are two SIMs active, I must also choose which is the **Default Voice Line** for any calls that I make and for SMS's (from **Settings -> Mobile**).

To make this choice, I tap the **Default Voice Line** field and tap to choose which of the active SIMs should be that default.

This will not stop calls from being made or received on the alternative SIM – and nor will it prevent texts to/from that SIM.

It simply sets the default to use when calling or messaging people for the first time.

What do I mean by that?

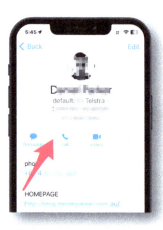

In general if I have previously called or texted a Contact using, say, my Telstra SIM, the next time I call or text (SMS) them, my device will use that same SIM in preference to the other – as long as that SIM is **On**.

If I have never called/texted that number before, the SIM identified by the Default Voice Line will be used. The Contact in the image on the right is such a contact – it will use the Default SIM.

Appendix D
Managing Multiple SIMs

For each contact, I can choose in the Contacts app which SIM should be used for the person – the 'Last Used' (which will be the Default Voice Line if there was no previous call) or whether all calls to that person should use a specific SIM.

For example, you may want all business calls to be made from your Business SIM – so can customise those Contacts.

When looking that the Contact's card, tap the words that appear beneath the contact name to see the options for Preferred Line (as shown on right).

If you have not specifically nominated a particular line/SIM for a contact, the **Last Used** will be the default setting – assuming that line is available. If not, then the Default Voice Line will be used.

When you dial a phone number from the Phone app, the Default Voice Line will show at the top if there are two active SIMs. Tap the line that is shown there to see and choose the line from which the call should be placed (see first image on right).

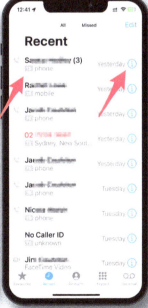

For calls that you make/receive, you will see, in the **Recent** option of the Phone app, the line that applied for the call and that will be used if you tap that number to call (see first image above). Again, this is only relevant if two SIMs are currently active.

In rightmost image above you can see under each name/ number that the TE (Telstra) phone line applied for each of these calls. If I tap the person's name or

Appendix D
Managing Multiple SIMs

phone number shown to call, the call will use the line shown (i.e. Telstra) – even if the Travel line is nominated as the default at the moment.

If you want to use a different line to that shown to call a Recent Contact, tap ⓘ on right of the call in Recent to see further details about the call.

The *Preferred Line* will again be shown under the person's name (like in Contacts) – see image on right.

Tap this to change your preference, which will apply the change for all future calls you make to that Contact (if that SIM is available).

In Messages, tap the profile circle at the top of a conversation to see the applicable **Conversation Line** (see image below), which will only be visible if there are two SIMs currently active below.

This shows which line is to be used when sending iMessages and Texts (SMSs) to the person.

Tap **Conversation Line** to the see the alternative line/SIM and to select that alternative SIM for future iMessages/texts with that person.

When starting a new Message using ✐ , you will see a **From** field under the **To** field at the top (once you have entered the name or number),

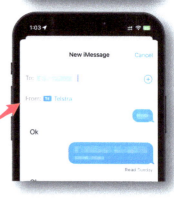

Appendix D
Managing Multiple SIMs

showing which line/SIM will be used for the Message. This applies to both new iMessages and new Text Messages.

Tap that **From** field to change the **Conversation Line** for the message.

Scenario 2: Two SIMs for phone/text, but disable mobile data

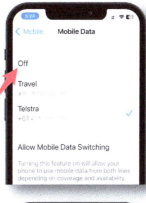

If I want to leave two SIMs enabled for calls and texts/messages, but don't want to risk using any mobile data, I simply tap the **Mobile Data** option at the top of **Settings -> Mobile** and choose **Off**.

I will also turn off **Data Roaming** for each SIM — so that I don't unintentionally use mobile data if I turn on mobile data for that SIM when outside my home country.

To do this, tap the applicable SIM under the **SIMs** heading.

Scroll down and turn off the **Data Roaming** switch.

With Data Roaming turned off, turning on Mobile Data for that SIM will only result in data usage if I am in my home country.

If I want to tightly control my data usage for my Travel SIM, I will do the same for that SIM.

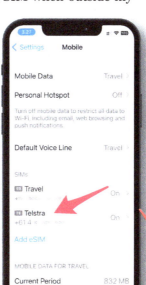

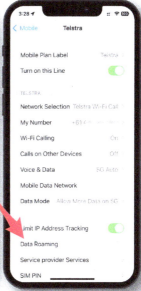

Scenario 3: Disable Home SIM and Only use Travel SIM

If I want to just use the Travel SIM for a period of time, I can simply tap on the Telstra SIM (in the section headed **SIMs**) and choose to disable (turn off) the **Turn on this Line** option.

Appendix D
Managing Multiple SIMs

I will always ensure that Data Roaming is turned off before I do this – so that, when I enable the SIM again while travelling (especially if I don't have another SIM active at that time) that I don't inadvertently end up using any mobile data.

The Default Voice Line for calls and SMSs will then be **Travel** (assuming that SIM is turned on). All calls and texts will use the Travel SIM's mobile number. iMessages that you send may also show as coming from this number (depending on your iMessage Settings).

If I want to use Mobile Data via the Travel SIM, I will tap Mobile Data and tap to tick and enable the Travel SIM.

If I am out of my home country and am sure that I want to use Data Roaming, I will then tap the SIM (under the **SIMs** section of **Settings -> Mobile**) and turn on the **Data Roaming** switch.

In **Settings -> Mobile**, I will also then scroll down to the app that I want to use and turn on the switch – to enable that app to use mobile internet. (This is assuming I have turned off all apps at the start of the trip as a precaution – as described on page 44.

When I am done using mobile data (and assuming I want to limit my use of Mobile Data), I will reverse all that. In **Settings -> Mobile**, I will turn off that app again, turn off Data Roaming for the SIM and set Mobile Data to **Off**.

If I have plenty of mobile data available for my Travel SIM, I will just leave Mobile Data and Data Roaming turned on – but still closely manage which apps can use it, to ensure I don't exceed the data limit provided.

For example I will, most of the time leave Messages, Facebook Messenger and WhatsApp turned on - so that I can receive any communications.

Scenario 4: Temporarily enable home SIM to receive an SMS

If I need to check for any SMS's sent to my home SIM, I tap on that SIM (under the SIMs section of **Settings -> Mobile**) and temporarily **Turn on this Line** for that SIM.

I quickly double-check that my Data Roaming is definitely OFF.

Any text messages (SMSs) that I have missed in the time that the SIM has been disabled will be received shortly after the line is turned on. This will not incur any cost.

Appendix D
Managing Multiple SIMs

If any call is received or made using that SIM/line when the SIM is enabled, or if I send an SMS using that SIM/line, there will be a cost incurred, as described earlier.

Once I have received my SMSs, I will turn my SIM back off by disabling **Turn on this Line**.

Scenario 5: Use Wi-Fi Calling with my home SIM

If I want to try using Wi-Fi Calling when connected to a Wi-Fi network to call and/or text those back home, I will first turn on my Telstra SIM, making sure that Data Roaming is turned off for that SIM.

I can then check if Wi-Fi Calling is available by tapping the SIM (under the **SIMs** section of **Settings -> Mobile**) and checking the **Network Selection** field, or by checking the Control Centre to see if the Wi-Fi Calling is now active. It may take a few minutes to activate. See page 23 for screen shots and further instructions.

If Wi-Fi Calling is available and if I want to be sure that calls or texts to home are from my Home SIM, I will turn off the Travel SIM temporarily.